The Agritopianists

THE AGRITOPIANISTS

THINKING AND PRACTICE IN RURAL JAPAN

Ou Ning

Translated by Matt Turner and Weng Haiying

The Center for Arts, Design, and Social Research
Boston · Helsinki

COVER: In the New Village at Moroyama, there are two posts written in Mushakoji Saneatsu's handwriting: "Those who pass through this gate (「この門に入るものは自己と他人の」) must respect themselves and all others (「生命を尊重しなければならない」)." Photo by Ou Ning, 2019.

CONTENTS

Preface vii

THE SPARK 2
WHITE BIRCH SOCIETY 13
ABIKO 30
THE IDEAL WORLD 41
NEW VILLAGE DEBATE 63
ECHOES IN CHINA 78
SECOND LIFE 99
POSTWAR YEARS 112
AGRICULTURAL FUNDAMENTALISM 135
SEMI-AGRICULTURAL LIFE 150
THE IHATOV 170
PATRON SAINT OF AGRICULTURE 184
THE TRUE WAY 193
THE AGRITOPIAS 214

Translators' Note 225

Glossary 227
References 237

Preface

This book could be regarded as the notes of a field trip. In October 2019, I made a research trip to study the Atarashiki-mura (New Village) Movement and other individual semi-agricultural life practices of Japanese writers and artists in the first half of the 20th century.

This is part of my ongoing research project on communitarian and utopian practices in different countries since the 19th century. I started this project in 2013, when I visited some hippie communes, intentional communities, and eco-villages in New Zealand. From there, I visited Denmark's Fristaden Christiania in 2014; Australia's "Rainbow Region," Nimbin, in 2015; American utopias such as the Oneida Community, Pleasant Hill Shaker Village, and New Harmony in 2016; Robert Owen's New Lanark in 2017; the historical site of Leonard and Dorothy Elmhirst's Dartington Experiment in 2018; and the ruins of Brook Farm in 2019. The Japan trip was my last "utopian" trip before Covid-19 broke out. I was lucky to make it with travel funds offered by the Center for Arts, Design, and Social Research (CAD+SR).

In the spring of 2019, I decided to write a book, *Utopia Field,* based on these research trips. After about half a year of quarantine because of the epidemic, my writing reached the peak of a blowout, as I finished nearly two hundred thousand Chinese words of a manuscript, in which the Japan chapter was the latest result. But it is not easy to find a publisher for the topic of "utopia" in China, so when CAD+SR started their publishing projects in 2021, I proposed to publish the English version of this Japan chapter as a test. Dalida Maria Benfield and Christopher Bratton, the founders of CAD+SR, agreed without the least hesitation, and I invited my friends Matt Turner and Weng Haiying as translators. This is where the book started.

Here, I would like to send my big thanks to Dalida and Christopher for their kindness and support. I would also like to thank Matt and Haiying for their precise and expressive translation. I am particularly grateful to XandC, the best graphic designers, who have worked with me for more than a decade on many publications, for their exquisite and cheerful design. Finally, my gratitude will go to Thomas Evans, who listed the book in the Artbook | D.A.P. catalogue, thus reaching more readers through its distribution network.

Ou Ning
16 July 2024

A railway crossing at the Hachiko Line, and a post in the distance that reads
Mushakoji Saneatsu and Atarashiki-mura Memorial Art Museum.
Photo by Ou Ning, 2019.

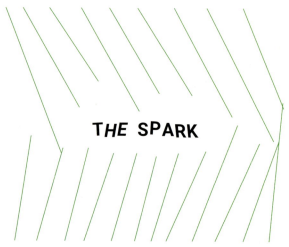

THE SPARK

Starting from the Japan Folk Crafts Museum in Komaba, Meguro, Tokyo, pass through Shinjuku and Ikebukuro to Sakado, transfer to the local commuter train in Saitama Prefecture, and arrive at Higashi-Moro Station in Iruma. After getting off, take a taxi to Moroyama. In total, it should take around two hours. In Saitama, advertisements for schools, nursing homes, cataract treatment centers, and funeral services are everywhere along the slow train route. According to a report in *The Asahi Shimbun* in 2012, the population of Saitama was still growing that year—although it also had the fastest rate of graying in Japan: "It is expected that the population will decline between 2015 and 2020."[1] Aging and the decline in births has been a population problem in Japan for many years. However, due to its geographical location in the Tokyo metropolitan area and relatively cheap cost of living, Saitama did not experience the expected population decline. Schools, especially language schools, can be seen everywhere—measures to attract international students, foreign workers, and encourage immigration. Nevertheless, its elderly population is significant.

My driver was an older man. He left me at a railway crossing on the Hachiko Line, where I saw a post in the distance that reads Mushakoji Saneatsu and Atarashiki-mura Memorial Art Museum. Across from the railway was a secluded path through the forest, with tall yew trees and low golden bamboo on either side. At the end of the forest was an open tea garden with rows of solar panels at its edge. An elderly woman was weeding and loosening the soil with a machine. On the left and right sides of the road, in the middle of a tea garden, there were two

---

[1]. *People's Daily*: Japan Channel, January 9, 2012. http://japan.people.com.cn/35467/7700384.html

more posts. On the right was written "Those who pass through this gate," and on the left side, "must respect themselves and all others"—in Mushakoji's handwriting. On the flat gravel-paved path were inlaid prominent yellow characters for Atarashiki-mura, meaning "New Village," which had faded over time. I was entering a graying village where the cinders of idealism had remained smoldering for over a century.

New Village at Moroyama was the second experimental base of the New Village Movement initiated by the writer Mushakoji Saneatsu. In 1918 (the seventh year of the Taisho era), he set up the first New Village in Kijo, Koyu District, Miyazaki Prefecture, Kyushu Island. Kijo was located within the territory of Hyuga, according to the geographical and administrative divisions of the time,[2] so it was also called New Village at Hyuga. In 1939 (the 14th year of the Showa Era), after New Village at Kijo was partially flooded by water diversion due to the construction of a reservoir by the local government,

---

[2] Between the Asuka and Meiji periods, the basic unit of Japan's geographical and administrative divisions was the Ryoseikoku (provincial) system, which was gradually replaced by Todofuken (prefectural, first level) and Shichoson (municipal, second level) system.

they found new land in Moroyama, at Tsuzuranuki,[3] near Tokyo, and moved New Village there. Moroyama is located in the Kanto region, so it was called New Village at Kanto. Today, there are still elderly members living there, but the number is very few (as of 2018, there were eight people in total).[4]

I walked past the tea garden and saw a pavilion on the left. In the pavilion, there was an old well. The wellhead was sealed, and there was also a water pump which was no longer used. A flagpole stood in front of the pavilion, and the village flag flapped in the wind, blue with the character for "field" (田) in the middle. The four squares of the field were yellow, black, red and white, which symbolized the saying that "all the peoples of the world are one family." I had heard there was a village song as well, but, so far, I was not able to find any information about it. The New Village emphasis on respect for life, and

---

3. Tsuzuranuki is regarded as a village at that time. In the administrative divisions of Japan, there are villages (*mura/son*, 大字), townships (*cho/machi*, 町) and urban townships (*shi*, 市) that make up basic local organizations; these are equivalent to China's 村, 乡, and 镇. Metropolis (*to*, 都), circuit/territory (*do*, 道), urban prefecture (*fu*, 府), and prefecture (*ken*, 県) are wide-area regional organizations.
4. "Mushakoji's Ideal Village: The 100th Anniversary Exhibition." *The Yomiuri Shimbun*, Morning Edition, October 30, 2018.

the world being one family, were humanitarian and cosmopolitan ideals formulated in the wake of the first World War.

Opposite the pavilion there was a small house. Replica handwriting of "The Spirit of New Village," by Mushakoji, hung at the door. This would be the visitor reception area of the New Village, but there was nobody there. There were two rooms inside, displaying several framed replicas of Mushakoji's handwriting, photos of him, and a few random objects. To the left, the New Village Life and Culture Museum covered an area of 200 square meters. It seemed mainly used to display historical photos, newspaper cuttings, as well as paintings, sculptures, ceramics, and literary works of members who lived in and outside the village. When it was in Kijo, New Village implemented two kinds of membership. One was for members of the village who lived at the base and practiced there, and the other was for members residing outside the village. Scattered across its many branches, they agreed with the spirit of New Village but did not participate in the collective life of the base, and only supported New Village with membership fees. As of 2013, New Village still had 160 members outside,[5] with the Tokyo branch becoming the leading force for maintaining New Village at Moroyama and organizing its many activities. The book *Centenary of New Village: 1918-2018* was displayed at the entrance to the museum, a document of their centenary commemoration on September 16, 2018. There was also a large poster of the centennial celebration inside the museum, on which there was a hand-painted aerial view of the New Village at Moroyama. The village flag flew in the center, bathed in sun. The surrounding farmland was flat, the village houses neatly arranged, the paths winding, the green dazzling, the white clouds in the sky elegant, and the city skyline in the distance, a mirage. This "ideal village" was a hermitage hidden near the city.

Around 100 meters from the reception desk, you could see a rebuilt version of the first wooden A-frame house erected when the New Village Movement began. Another hundred meters away was the Mushakoji Saneatsu Memorial Art Museum. A large stone was in front of the museum, carved with the well-known saying "Where is there no

---

5. The New Village Foundation: http://atarashiki-mura.or.jp/gaiyo/

beauty?" Entering the front yard, I could see Takata Hiroatsu's sculpture, "Worship," a female figure cast in bronze. There was also a plaque on the lintel of the art museum that read "I might as well be happy" in Mushakoji's handwriting. Takata was a friend of Mushakoji's. During the Taisho era, he created a communal village at Shimo-Takaido. He also serialized the translation of Michelangelo's letters in *Shirakaba* ("White Birch") magazine and participated in an art exhibition organized by Mushakoji. Later, while living in France, he befriended Romain Rolland, Jean Cocteau, and others. His sculptures were donated to the village in 1982. There was an elderly woman on duty at the art museum, selling tickets for 200 yen. The museum covers an area of 250 square meters. It was built in 1980 and displays over 400 original paintings and calligraphy works, literary manuscripts, and publications by Mushakoji, as well as works by his friends: Nagayo Yoshiro, Senge Motomaro, Kurata Hyakuzo, Nakagawa Kazumasa, Tsubaki Sadao, Kohno Michisei, Zhou Zuoren and others. Here, and the Chofu Mushakoji Saneatsu Memorial Museum, are the two places with the most complete collections of documents on the

New Village Movement in Japan, sometimes lending out to other institutions for exhibition.

Opposite the museum was a 580-square-meter public hall. On its exterior wall was painted the character "田" of the village flag, and a hand-painted map of the village hung at the door. In the public hall there was a meeting room, an office, an activity room, a stage, a canteen, and a bathroom. Members could enjoy three meals a day there free of charge or take meals back to their residences. This was also the primary place for annual routine activities, such as the birthday celebration of Mushakoji in May, the Flower Festival in July, Labor Day in August, and the anniversary ceremony every September. Members inside and outside the village would first gather there, and then go outdoors to participate in activities. Also, the Tokyo branch often holds firefly watching parties and taro cooking parties there. They can stay in an outside member's area at night. The public hall typically sells eggs, mushrooms, rice, vegetables, tea, yuzu, ginkgo, bamboo shoots, and bamboo charcoal, among other things produced by the village; a signboard there advertises "pesticide free" as a selling point. Ideas of environmental protection in the community keep pace with the times, as was apparent in the adoption of solar panels, proof of their acceptance of new energy technologies.

The New Village at Moroyama owns 10 hectares of land and has 3 hectares of leased land.[6] When viewed as a satellite image, it is a parallelogram extending from the southwest to the northeast. In the west are the Chichibu Mountains. In addition to the tea garden, reception room, the two museums, and the public hall, there are also houses, workshops, and chicken coops. Also worth seeing is the decommissioned Toden 7022 (Tokyo tram car) donated by members outside the village in 1968, which at one point was used as a kindergarten classroom for the village. In addition, there is the village funerary hall. After his death in 1976, the ashes of Mushakoji were placed there. His tomb is located in the central cemetery of Tobukimachi, Hachioji.

In the New Village at Moroyama, I saw only four people from the beginning to end of my visit. The weeders in the tea garden, the gallery staff, and the people on duty in the public hall were all

---

6. Ibid.

older women. There was also an elderly man whom I saw returning to the village from a wooded area. Because I don't speak Japanese, I couldn't really talk much with them. A brief visitor, I saw only a sleepy village. But, in fact, its heart still beats tenaciously. In the art museum, I saw that the official publication of the New Village Movement, *New Village*, was still published in Moroyama. It has published 72 volumes since 1918 (as of 2020). Before 2018, it was monthly, but after 2019 it was changed to a quarterly. Although each issue is printed in 13 x 18.5 cm in monotone, and is thin, with only 20 or 30 pages, it carefully tends a flame that has burned for a century. Although the two elderly women in the art museum and the public hall could not answer my questions, they warmly called a taxi for me. When the car drove out of the woods and back into the outside world, the image of the "utopia" depicted on the centennial celebration poster was still in my mind. Beautiful and dreamlike, it pushed me to explore more.

The Shirakaba Literary Museum, Abiko.
Photo by Ou Ning, 2019.

WHITE BIRCH SOCIETY

Mushakoji Saneatsu was born on May 12, 1885 (the 18th year of the Meiji era). His father, Mushakoji Saneyo, was awarded a viscount the previous year because of his contributions to commerce, law, and politics. Therefore, his family belonged to the "aristocrats" (Kazoku) who had performed meritorious deeds in the past.[1] He was two when his father died of tuberculosis, and his maternal uncle, Kadenokoji Sukekoto, temporarily took over his father's position. At the age of six, he was sent

---

1. The Kazoku were a class of nobility established in Japan in 1884 (17th year of the Meiji era) through the promulgation of the "Kazoku Order," which was abolished in 1947 (22nd year of the Showa era) with the Constitution of Japan.

to the elite Gakushuin Peers School,[2] where he remained until he entered Tokyo Imperial University at the age of 21. While an upperclassman, influenced by his uncle, he began to read a large number of Leo Tolstoy's works in Japanese translation, instilling in him the desire to "de-aristocratize." He became close friends with his classmate Shiga Naoya, and the two had a good relationship with an alum of the school, Arishima Takeo, who had returned from studying at Harvard University. Through him, they were introduced to Walt Whitman's poetry. They also went "backpacking" before graduating, from Mount Fuji in Yamanashi Prefecture to Mount Akagi in Gunma Prefecture, to experience the life of the poor on foot.[3]

While at Tokyo Imperial University, Mushakoji

---

[2] The name Gakushuin dates back to the Heian Period (8th century, CE), when Emperor Saga and Empress Danrin (Tachibana no Kachiko) established a private school for the sons in the imperial family. In 1847, during the Edo period, Emperor Ninko established a school for court nobles in the Kyoto Imperial Palace. In 1876 (9th year of the Meiji era), the school was renamed the Gakushujo, and the following year the school was renamed Kazoku Gakko, or Peers School. The school provided a complete education from kindergarten through elementary school, high school to university.

[3] "The Life of Saneatsu," *Chofu Mushakoji Saneatsu Museum Catalog* (1994), pp. 9-13.

studied social sciences and Shiga studied English. On April 14, 1907, they formed the 14th Day Club with Ogimachi Kinkazu and Kinoshita Rigen, and published the magazine *Nozono* to showcase their writings. At almost the same time, a younger student of the academy, Satomi Ton (younger brother of Arishima Takeo; who took the name Yamanouchi Hideo after his adoption by his maternal grandfather; with a pen name of Satomi Ton), published the journal *Wheat*, while Yanagi Soetsu and Kori Torahiko were publishing *Peach Garden*. Shiga's diary shows that on October 18, 1907, in a hotel in Fujisawa, Kanagawa, he and Mushakoji planned to start a new magazine, and invited people to participate.[4] Starting in 1908, around a dozen students at Peers School donated two yen per month to prepare the new magazine. In April 1910, the three student magazines were combined into one, and a new magazine named *Shirakaba*, highly influenced by Russian literature, was published by Rakuyodo. The White Birch Society of Modern Japanese Literature was born.

---

4. *The Complete Works of Shiga Naoya*, Vol. 10: Diary (Tokyo: Iwanami Shoten, 1973). "Kanagawa Literature Chronology (Meiji 31-45)," Kanagawa Museum of Modern Literature. https://www.kanabun.or.jp/material-data/chronological-table/chronological-table-04/

In the table of contents of the inaugural issue of *Shirakaba*, first is a review of the novel *And Then* written by Natsume Soseki, the great master of Meiji literature, authored by Mushakoji. The issue also includes "The New Idealism in German Painting" by Kojima Kikuo (who designed the cover of the issue and signed it "KK San"); the new-style poem "In Rome" by Arishima Ikuma (brother of Arishima Takeo); another new-style poem, "The Song of Heaviness," also by Mushakoji; the tanka "The New Belt" by Kinoshita Rigen; a summary of *Elektra* by Hugo von Hofmannsthal, as translated by Kori Torahiko; the Anton Chekhov story "The Family Meeting" as translated by Satomi Ton; the Henryk Sienkiewicz story "Quo Vadis" as translated by Arishima Takeo; the story "As Far as Abashiri" by Shiga Naoya; the story "The General Store" by Ogimachi Kinkazu; the inaugural statement and news by "Journalists" (Mushakoji, Shiga, Satomi Ton, Yanagi Soetsu); and, finally, an illustration section introducing European artworks.[5] From the beginning, *Shirakaba* had a strong international flavor, and not only published literary works, but also paid

---

5. See reproductions in *Shirakaba* (Kyoto: Rinsen Shoten, 1965).

substantial attention to new art. Before its suspension in 1923, it held 12 art exhibitions in total, introducing to Japan a wide range of original works of European modern art, including works of Impressionism, Post-Impressionism, Fauvism, Expressionism, and Cubism. This fostered the strength of Japanese art and artists—not only affecting the growth of Japanese modern art, but also triggering the subsequent Japanese Folk Craft Movement.

In the same year as the birth of the White Birch Society, the Japan-Korea Annexation Treaty was signed, signaling the collapse of the Korean Empire, and formally establishing it as a Japanese colony. Two bloody battles—between Japan and the Qing Dynasty in China, and Japan and Russia—seemed to be settled, but Northeast Asia was still roiling. That year, the plague struck northeast China, killing more than 60,000 people; the socialist Kotoku Shusui, who later became an anarchist, published "The 20th Century Monster of Imperialism," was accused of conspiring to assassinate the Meiji Emperor; and the Japanese government launched a large-scale search and arrest, known as the High Treason Incident. Prior to that, Wang Jingwei organized the attempted assassination of the Qing Prince Regent Zaifeng in Beijing, which led to the Gengxu Bomb Incident; and Liu Shifu and others set up the Chinese Assassination Corps with the goal of assassinating Yuan Shikai. This was an era when anarchists frequently enacted the "propaganda of deed" and carried out revolutionary mobilization through political assassinations. Wang Jingwei was saved from death because of the kindness of the chief judge on his case, Shan Qi. But Kotoku Shusui was sentenced to death the following year; his death was regarded by many Japanese intellectuals as "entrapment." Even Shiga Naoya, who did not care for politics, wrote articles in outrage against Mikado nationalism. These children of the aristocracy, who enjoyed every privilege, went through a baptism of individualism, liberalism, humanitarianism, and cosmopolitanism with a broad international vision. They were not afraid to be seen as heretics and felt they should speak out in their publications. Peers School regarded them as "good-for-nothings" and listed *Shirakaba* as forbidden.

As one of the founders and a core member of the White Birch Society, Mushakoji held a negative view of the compulsory military service established by Yamagata Aritomo, the "father of militarism."[6] Mushakoji no longer had any respect for General Nogi Maresuke, the director of Peers School at the time, the exemplar of the "bushido model"[7] as represented by the worship of the emperor (the Mikado) and the national religion of Shinto. He once said, in front of Nogi, that "soldiers do not know the value of human beings."[8] Shiga Naoya and Satomi Ton, as well as Nagayo Yoshiro, who joined the White Birch Society in 1911, were in deep agreement. Yanagi Soetsu had been studying and collecting folk

---

[6] It is said that the High Treason Incident was framed by Yamagata Aritomo, as Kotoku Shusui's newspaper *Yoruzuchoho* revealed the truth about the Japanese army's participation in the Eight-Power Allied Forces in China in 1900, plundering silver. According to Ian Baruma, Yamagata Aritomo's "most important legacy was the role of the Imperial Armed Forces. The idea of a national army of conscripts was revolutionary in a country where carrying arms had been the privilege of a military caste." Ian Baruma, *Inventing Japan: 1853-1964* (New York: The Modern Library, 2004), p. 54.

[7] Nogi Maresuke, who participated in the Satsuma Rebellion, the Sino-Japanese War, the Japanese invasion of Taiwan, and Russo-Japanese War, served as governor of Taiwan from 1896 to 1898 and as director of Peers School from 1907 to 1912. In 1912, after the Meiji Emperor died, he and his wife committed *seppuku*.

[8] Nagayo Yoshiro, *The Journey of My Heart* (Tokyo: Chikuma Shobo, 1959), p. 155. The translation is cited in Liu Lishan, *Japanese Writers of the White Birch Society and Chinese Writers* (Shenyang: Liaoning University Press, 1995), p. 109.

artifacts from the Joseon period of Korea, and was very indignant about the Japan-Korea Treaty and the subsequent suppression of the Korean independence movement by Japan: "If one takes General Nogi as a model and wants to be a righteous minister like him, then the Koreans have no choice but to fight against Japan."[9] Arishima Takeo discovered Peter Kropotkin's thought while studying at Harvard in 1903. When he returned to Japan in 1907, he made a special detour to London to visit the exile, and sent a letter on behalf of Kropotkin to Kotoku Shusui. He himself became one of the earliest popularizers of Kropotkin's anarchism in Japan.[10] Although the White Birch Society was not a political group per se, these writers and artists were closely watching the changes taking place across the world. In the "age of blockage" (a term first used by Ishikawa Takuboku in 1910) triggered by the High Treason

---

[9] Ubukata Naokichi, "The Japanese View of Korea through Yanagi Soetsu," *Thought* (448, Oct. 1961), pp. 66-77. The translation is cited in Liu Lishan, *Japanese Writers of the White Birch Society and Chinese Writers*, p. 180.

[10] Yasukawa Sadao, *Tragedy of the Intellectuals: Arishima Takeo* (Tokyo: Shintensha, 1983), pp. 72, 262. Cited in Liu Lishan, p. 73.

Incident,[11] the previous Naturalism (*Shizenshugi*) and Aestheticism (*Tanbi-ha*) gave way to the New Idealism (*Shinrisoshugi*) of the White Birch Society. They all left Tokyo Imperial University, and afterward their social thought was honed through literary practice and the wider troubled world that was approaching them.

After entering the second decade of the 20th century, major events arrived one after another. In 1911, the Xinhai Revolution broke out in China, and the Republic of China—the first republic in Asia—was founded on the following New Year's Day. In 1912, the Meiji Emperor died and Japan entered the Taisho era. In 1914, the First World War broke out because of nationalist disputes and conflicts over colonies and world markets. With confidence built by the First Sino-Japanese War and the Russo-Japanese War, Japan, intending to reap greater benefits in China and the Western Pacific, decided to join the Allied countries and declare war on the Central Powers, becoming the first participating country

---

[11] Ishikawa Takuboku, "The Present Age of Blockage: The Last of the Autocrats and Pure Naturalism, and an Investigation into Tomorrow" (1910) in *The Complete Works of Japanese Literature (12): Kunikida Doppo–Ishikawa Takuboku Collection* (Tokyo: Shueisha, 1967). https://www.aozora.gr.jp/cards/000153/files/814_20612.html

outside of Europe. Japan immediately seized the German concession at Qingdao. The Republic of China, whose foundation was unstable, had been bullied on its sovereign territory, but had to remain neutral. It had neither soldiers, nor guns, nor money, nor warships. However, Liang Shiyi, a former Qing Dynasty scholar from Sanshui, Foshan, Guangdong Province, and a minister under Yuan Shikai, proposed "substituting workers for soldiers," allowing France, Britain and Russia to accept 300,000 Chinese workers on European battlefields. They were organized as the Chinese Labor Corps (CLC) to provide labor services, making China a nominal participant in the war. This ensured the weak Beiyang government's participation in armistice negotiations and post-war decisions.[12] In 1917, the October Revolution took place in Russia, and the first socialist country was established. In 1918, at the end of the war,

---

12. Mark O'Neill, *The Chinese Labour Corps: The Forgotten Chinese Labourers of the First World War* (Melbourne: Penguin Books, 2014), pp. 5-9. The Beiyang government was the internationally recognized government of the Republic of China between 1912 and 1928, based in Beijing. It was dominated by the generals of the Beiyang Army, giving it its name.

the Rice Riots occurred in Japan.[13] In 1919, when the Paris Peace Conference was held, the Beiyang government objected to Japan's proposed Article 21 and demanded that Japan withdraw its troops from Shandong. The failure to do so triggered the May 4th Movement, which inaugurated the historical narrative of China's modern nationalism.[14] At the Peace Conference, Woodrow Wilson put forward the principle of national self-determination against colonialism which contributed to the rise of the post-war independence movement of nation-states, including the March 1st Movement in Korea. This preceded the May 4th Movement by two months, with both of the protest movements targeting Japan.

The thread of history has long been submerged

---

[13] The Rice Riots of 1918 were a series of popular disturbances that erupted throughout Japan from July to September 1918, which brought about the collapse of the Terauchi Masatake administration.

[14] The Japanese historian Miyawaki Junko argues that "China's semi-colonization did not begin with the Opium War" and sets the beginning of China's modern history as the First Sino-Japanese War. In her view, the "humiliation" that Japan visited on the Qing Dynasty and the study of post-Meiji Restoration Japan by Chinese intellectuals had a significant impact on the formation of the Chinese nation-state and its modernization. She also disagrees with the view that the May 4th Movement was the beginning of Chinese nationalism. Miyawaki Junko, *This is the True History of China: 1840-1949* (New Taipei City: Gusa Press, 2015), pp. 41-44, 208-217.

in time's folds. Geopolitical conflict and turbulence often change the course of people's lives. Y. C. James Yen (Yan Yangchu), a volunteer from the YMCA, helped the CLC as they paved railways, built military ports, dug trenches, filled sandbags and carried corpses on Europe's battlefields. He helped them write letters home and taught them to read—which became the starting point for his later mass education and rural reconstruction movement in China and the Philippines. In 1916, when the Battle of the Somme broke out, with an eventual 1.34 million casualties, Mushakoji was misdiagnosed as having tuberculosis.[15] He moved to Abiko with his wife Takeo Fusako, whom he had married three years earlier, to recuperate, turning it into an activity base for the White Birch Society. The brutality of the war, the establishment of the Soviet regime in Russia, the tragic struggle for survival in the Rice Riots, together with his own physical illness and a low point in his literary career, germinated a utopian idea in his mind. In May 1918, he wrote three "dialogues about a new village." The first was serialized in

---

15. "A Brief Chronology of Mushakoji Saneatsu," *Chofu Mushakoji Saneatsu Museum Catalogue*, (1994), p. 93.

Osaka Daily News with the title of "A Country." The second and third were published in *Shirakaba* as "Beginning the New Life."[16] In July, *New Village* was launched; in September, the general area of the site was determined, in Hyuga. He started from Abiko and went to Tokyo, Hamamatsu, Matsumoto, Kyoto, Osaka, Kobe, and Fukuoka to preach the New Village plan. He recruited more than 300 members, and in October inspected and purchased land in Hyuga. On November 14, he and five adults, along with two children—a total of eight people— arrived at Kijo, Koyu District, Miyazaki Prefecture, and established the first New Village.[17] It happened that three days prior, on November 11, Germany and France ended hostilities, and the First World War concluded.

In April of the year 1918, the 100th issue of *Shirakaba* was published and celebrated in Tokyo. The social influence of the White Birch Society in

---

[16] These three dialogues express Mushakoji's theories and visions of New Village in the style of Socratic questioning. The second and third were published in May and June 1918, while the first was published in July. They were put in chronological order when later collected in *The Life of New Village* (Tokyo: Shinchosha, 1918).

[17] "A Brief Chronology of Mushakoji Saneatsu," *Chofu Mushakoji Saneatsu Museum Catalogue*, p. 93.

Japan was now at its peak. The competition between nations and the political issues raised by the First World War triggered people's unprecedented desire to express themselves, while Japan's short-term economic prosperity brought by war dividends, the rise of the universal suffrage movement, and the loosened social atmosphere of the so-called "Taisho democracy" provided the conditions for the expansion of the publishing industry. Many satellite magazines appeared around *Shirakaba*, triggering the additional Shinshu (now Nagano) White Birch Movement in the central region of Honshu. Mushakoji, Arishima Takeo, Kishida Ryusei, and Yanagi Soetsu were frequently invited there for local literary and arts events. But the works of the White Birch Society were not only widely read in Japan, they also spread to China. Zhou Zuoren paid close attention to the White Birch Society during his time studying in Japan, and continued to receive the magazine by mail after returning to China in 1911. He published his impressions of the play, "A Dream of a Youth," by Mushakoji in *New Youth* in May 1918—which aroused Lu Xun's interest. Lu Xun then translated the full text of the play and published it in *New Youth* from January to April, 1920. Later, the Zhou brothers continued to translate and introduce the works of Arishima Takeo, Nagayo Yoshiro, Shiga Naoya, Senge Motomaro and other works of Mushakoji, which were included in *Selection of Modern Japanese Fiction* (Shanghai: The Commercial Press, 1923), *Two Traces of Blood* (Shanghai: Kaiming Books, 1927), and *Translations at the Wall* (Shanghai: Beixin Books, 1929). China's enthusiasm for translations of the White Birch Society lasted until several years after the ending of the publication of *Shirakaba*.

In 1923, Arishima Takeo and his lover Hatano Akiko, a journalist for *Women's Review*, committed double suicide at the Arishima family villa, "Jogetsuan," in Mikasa, Karuizawa, Nagano. The Kanto earthquake happened, affecting Tokyo Prefecture, Kanagawa Prefecture, Chiba Prefecture and Shizuoka Prefecture, resulting in the collapse of nearly 130,000 buildings. The fire caused by the earthquake destroyed nearly 450,000 houses, and more than 140,000 people were killed or missing. Another famous Japanese anarchist, and the translator of Kropotkin's *Mutual Aid*, Osugi Sakae, was killed in the chaos of the earthquake along with his wife Ito Noe and his nephew Tachibana

Soichi. An officer in the Imperial Japanese Army, Amakasu Masahiko, took advantage of the situation in what is known as the Amakasu Incident. After 13 years of existence and 160 issues, *Shirakaba* reached its end because of this disaster. At the same time, the publication of the left-wing literary magazine *The Seeder*, which had only been around for two years, was suspended. However, its successor, *Literary Front*, was soon published in 1924. The Proletarian Literature aka New Realism (*Shingenjitsushugi*) that it promoted displaced the status of the White Birch Society. However, in the same year, thanks to the efforts of Mushakoji, Shiga, Senge, and Kurata, the successor to *Shirakaba*—*Buji*—appeared. The influence of the White Birch Society as a literary group has gradually declined. So it is amazing that, as a branch growing from its trunk, the utopian practices of the New Village have continued tenaciously to this day.

The post pointing to Mushakoji Saneatsu's former residence, Abiko.
Photo by Ou Ning, 2019.

ABIKO

Abiko is located 50 kilometers north of Tokyo. From the southern entrance of JR Station, you can see a sign fixed onto granite slate, introducing "relevant cultural figures of Abiko." On it, there is a magnified photo of Mushakoji Saneatsu, Shiga Naoya, Yanagi Soetsu and their families on the 32nd birthday of Mushakoji, in 1917. Because the three core figures of the White Birch Society once lived here, during the Taisho era, at the time, Abiko was also known as "Kamakura of the North"—mirroring the literary city of Kamakura, 60 kilometers to the south of Tokyo. In 2001, the Shirakaba Literary Museum was opened with the support of Sano Riki,[1] President of Oracle Japan. As the White Birch archive, it connects the former residences of Mushakoji, Shiga, and Yanagi as a literary map of Abiko. However, compared with Kamakura's literary tourism resources, the city offers little. The former residences of Mushakoji and Yanagi are currently private and not open to the public. Shiga's former residence is the only open site, and within it, only a former study has been restored for visiting.

The first one to settle in Abiko was Yanagi's uncle Kano Jigoro, who was the president of Tokyo Higher Normal School, president of the Kobun Institute, and the founder of Judo. In 1911, Kano came to build villas and establish a farm. In 1914, he invited his newly married nephew, Yanagi Soetsu, and his wife, Nakajima Kaneko, to move there. The period when they lived in Abiko was crucial for Yanagi to launch his Folk Craft Movement later on.

---

[1] Sano Riki graduated from Otaru University of Commerce in 1963, and since 2000 he has been studying his alumnus, Kobayashi Takiji, a representative writer of Japanese Proletarian Literature who was heavily influenced by the White Birch Society. This led to Sano's decision to preserve the literary heritage of the White Birch Society for future generations.

It began with the White Birch Society contacting the French sculptor Auguste Rodin. In 1910, in order to prepare the "Rodin special issue" of *Shirakaba*, Arishima Ikuma wrote to Rodin to commission him and sent him 30 Ukiyo-e prints. In return, Rodin sent him three small sculptures for *Shirakaba*, which were kept in Yanagi Soetsu's home in Abiko. In 1914, a young Japanese man who was a primary school teacher in Japan-occupied Korea, sculptor Asakawa Noritaka, went to see these. As a gift, he gave Yanagi an underglaze blue and white porcelain pot with autumn grass patterns from the Joseon period in Korea. Yanagi was immediately fascinated by Korean craftwork. From then on, he regularly went to Korea to investigate Buddhist statuary and porcelain work, and gradually transformed from the modern art critic of the White Birch Society into a scholar of folk handicrafts. Later, in 1925, he coined the term "folk craft" (*mingei*) in Wakayama with Hamada Shoji and Kawai Kanjiro, launching the Folk Craft Movement. Handicrafts that he collected in Korea from the Goreyo and Joseon periods are stored and displayed at the Japan Folk Crafts Museum he founded at Komaba, Meguro, Tokyo.

Today, Kano's villa in Abiko is no more, though the former residence of Yanagi Sanjuso, the Three Trees Manor, is well-preserved. It was made in the traditional Japanese thatched style of Gassho-style houses, with the roof placed like two hands in prayer, but the grass roof was replaced with glazed tiles. It is named for the three ancient chestnut trees in the courtyard. The property now belongs to Waka poet and local historian Murayama Shoho. Because the gate is closed, it is difficult to see inside. The high point where the Three Trees Manor is located is called Tenjinyama Ryokuchi Park, which overlooks the vast waters of Lake Teganuma, the largest lake in Abiko. There is a tree-lined footpath to the front gate, where a sign says "Tenjinzaka," denoting the hill path. When you climb down the steps, you can see a plaque written by Murayama Shoho commemorating the three members of the White Birch Society who lived in the town. After descending the mountain, walk about 300 meters to the left, and you will find the Shirakaba Literary Museum. Walk 50 meters further, and you will find the ruins of Shiga Naoya's former residence.

The Shirakaba Literary Museum is a small

building with three floors and a basement, designed by Sano Kei. At the entrance, there is a U-shaped marble sculpture, *Be a Refuge unto Yourself*, through which the artist Sazi Masahiro pays tribute to the White Birch writers. The title is taken from a couplet of Shakyamuni's, one line of which is "Be a Lamp unto Yourself." To the left on the first floor is the exhibition hall, and on the right is the library, which has a very thorough collection of publications related to the White Birch Society and the New Village Movement. To the left on the second floor is the Japanese-style multipurpose room, and on the right is the second exhibition hall, which mainly displays letters, manuscripts, and rare editions of White Birch books. One item is a letter from Arishima Takeo to Shiga Naoya, in elegant handwriting. There is a music room in the basement, which mainly displays the records and musical scores of Nakajima Kaneko (who took the name Yanagi Kaneko after marriage; she is regarded as the "mother of Japanese vocal music" and famous for her bel canto). A spiral staircase runs through all floors, up from the basement. A third floor is not open to the public. Because of its small scale, I could record all the materials in the library after browsing the exhibitions.

The site of Shiga's former residence is hidden in a dense forest alongside the road. It takes a few steps before you see it through an opening in the shade. There lies a lonely wooden study to the left, on a very small scale. The explanatory text next to it indicates that it is a reproduction. The original main house is very large, and Shiga built this small study independent of the main house in order to focus on his writing. He moved to Abiko in 1915 at the instigation of Mushakoji. His relationship with his father had long been tense, especially after his marriage in 1914 to Mushakoji's cousin, Kadenokoji Yasuko, as Kadenokoji had been widowed and then remarried. This was strongly opposed by his father. So, he moved there with his wife to live independently. Most of his representative works, such as *At Kinosaki*, *Reconciliation*, *The Shopboy's God* and *A Dark Night's Passing*, were completed in this small study—these made him the "Novel God" of Japanese literary history. In 1916, he and Yanagi persuaded Mushakoji and his wife to move and join them. That same year, the British ceramicist Bernard Leach, the only foreign member of the White Birch

Society, was invited by Yanagi to join the group and set up a kiln to make pottery at Three Trees Manor.

It takes a little over 20 minutes to walk from the site of Shigo's former residence to Mushakoji's former residence. The latter is also located along the coast of Lake Teganuma. Yanagi, Shiga, and Leach were in the east and Mushakoji was in the west. They walked or took boats across Lake Teganuma to meet each other. The sky was high and there were rarely clouds, the fields were open, the trees were verdant, the water and grasses lush, and the boats thronged. They were all children of aristocratic families, and their big houses were located in places with similarly grand views and beautiful scenery. Mushakoji's home was at the west end of the Boatmen's Forest, a dense, old-growth forest, a protected green zone. When I finally located the house, I found that I could see nothing except for the monument and signs at the front gate. The closed courtyard door and the surrounding trees completely obscured the building. After he set up New Village in Kijo in 1918, he sold the house in August 1919 because of the urgent need for funds, and all the 5000 yen he gained from the sale was used to invest in his utopian project.

Who is the property owner now? In 2019, news appeared from Abiko, referring to Sankyo Frontier, the caretakers of the Mushakoji house. They would be opening it to the public for two days, from November 22 to 23, of this year; appointments were needed.[2] This was after I visited.

Mushakoji was the last to move in and the first to leave. In 1919, Leach left because of a fire in his pottery studio, which destroyed all his work and materials. In 1920, he said goodbye to Japan and returned to Britain. Yanagi moved back to Tokyo in 1921. Shiga didn't leave for Kyoto until 1923. During their stay in Abiko, other artists and writers of the White Birch Society—such as Kishida Ryusei, Inukai Ken, Umehara Ryuzaburo, Abe Yoshishige, Nagayo Yoshiro, and others—visited frequently. Mushakoji also launched preparations for the establishment of

---

[2] "Special Exhibition at Mushakoji Saneatsu's Former Residence:" https://www.abikoinfo.jp/mushanokouji-release/. Sankyo Frontier Group is a Japanese group of companies dedicated to building prefabricated parts and mobile construction materials, with branches in several countries: https:// sankyofrontier-global.com

the Shirakaba Art Museum.[3] But in the first half of 1918, he must have been completely occupied by the New Village. He wrote: "This thought, that thought, I don't believe that what I think is wrong. I fully believe in myself, and in my determination to build a world like this. I'm passionate about keeping pace with the times. I believe that if there are 50 or 60 people, no, 20 or 30 people, I think it can be realized. The more that people laugh at the impossibility of this, and the naivety of this kind of vague thinking, and the more I believe it possible. The idea of showing this to everybody—it's like a burning flame."[4] Finally, on September 15 of that year, around 50 members of the White Birch Society, and members of the New Village, attended a grand

---

[3] The Shirakaba Art Museum was not yet built at that time. In order to fulfill Mushakoji's last wishes, the owner of the Yoshii Gallery in Ginza, Yoshii Chozo, who was associated with the White Birch Society, bought the site of the abandoned Kiyoharu Elementary School in 1981 in Yamanashi, Hokuto, Nagasaka, and turned it into the Kiyoharu Art Colony. In 1983, he established the Kiyoharu Shirakaba Museum, mainly collecting paintings and manuscripts of the White Birch Society, their associates, and other documents.

[4] "Dialogue on New Village," by Mushakoji Saneatsu, translated by Sun Baigang, *New Village* (Shanghai: Guanghua Book Company, 1933), p. 46; translated from Mushakoji Saneatsu, *Life in New Village* (Tokyo: Shinchosha, 1918).

farewell party at his home in Abiko. He recorded the moment: "The sunset is beautiful… Under the reflection of the clouds, it dyes the Teganuma gold. It's so quiet and magnificent. Even though I've lived here for two years, I've never seen it like this. This is a sign of fate."[5] From that time on, he dedicated his life to the building of New Village.

---

5. *Selected Works of Mushakoji Saneatsu* (Tokyo: Sedousha, 1964), p. 447.

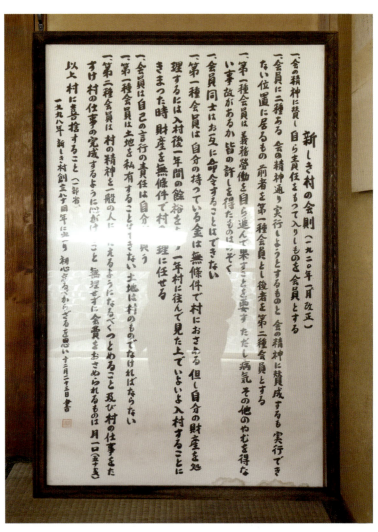

The 1998 copy of the 1920 New Village Rules, in the visitor reception room, Moroyama.
Photo by Ou Ning, 2019.

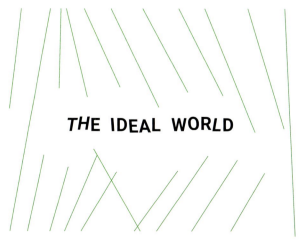

THE IDEAL WORLD

The place where the New Village at Kijo was located is called Ishikawauchi, which is the site of a stone castle from the Sengoku period. To its rear is the green Mount Osuzu. It is a three-tiered area, called upper castle, middle castle, and lower castle by locals. The second level extends down to the Omaru River, at the mountain's foot. The water of the Omaru wraps around three sides in the shape of a horseshoe, making it appear as a peninsula and isolating it from the outside world. When entering the village, you need to cross the river by boat. In the rainy season, the river is as wide as 15 meters. The depth of the river during this time is unknown and travel across it is extremely inconvenient. Even in today's satellite images, the surrounding area is still green, and human traces are rare—an area even more remote over a century ago. The Ishikawauchi Dam, built in 1938, is located upstream of Omaru, north of the New Village of Kijo. There is also a small dam in the river section where the village is located. The submerged "lower castle" stills show an outline in the dry season. There is a natural boulder in middle of the Omaru, named Rodin Rock—the symbol of New Village at that time—but it is now submerged. After New Village moved from Kijo to Moroyama that year, there were still two members, Sugiyama and Takahashi, who remained. Until 2018, three people still lived there.[1] Now the "upper castle" features the restored house where Mushakoji lived, a relatively simple Mushakoji Saneatsu Memorial Museum. Although the New Village at Kijo is listed as a protected cultural heritage site, due to its remote location, the number of visitors is less than that of New Village at Moroyama.

Zhou Zuoren was the first Chinese to visit

---

[1] "Saneatsu's Ideal World: Centenary Exhibition," *Yomiuri Shimbun*, Morning Edition, October 30, 2018.

the New Village at Kijo. He became interested in Mushakoji through reading *Shirakaba* and became a subscriber. He was the first to write an article about Mushakoji's New Village Movement in China, and also established the New Village branch in Beijing in 1920. In his "Visit to Japan's New Village," published in the October 1919, Volume 2, No. 1 issue of *The Renaissance,* he described his difficult journey from Beijing to Tanggu, Tianjin, on July 2 of that year. He traveled by steamboat to Mojiko Station, then by train to Yoshimatsu in Kagoshima, and then on to Fukushima in Miyazaki. From there, he went by coach to Takanabe, then to Takajo, where he was picked up by Mushakoji, and crossed mountain after mountain in the rain, before finally arriving at the New Village of Kijo on the evening of July 7.[2] Today's transportation may be much more convenient and faster than at that time, but because it is so far away from Tokyo (it took three days to travel from Tokyo when the New Village was founded), I backed off and gave up on my plan of visiting.

    Mushakoji originally wanted to locate New

---

[2]   Zhou Zuoren, "Visit to Japan's New Village," *Art and Life* (Beijing: October Literature and Art Press, 2011), pp. 244-249.

Village near Tokyo, but he could not find a suitably rural setting. In order to implement Tolstoy's pan-laborism, he had to go to the countryside. Although the road to Kijo was long, he was nevertheless very excited when he arrived: "One morning in December 1918, I walked to the river. The clear water rushed against the rocks, overflowing with foam. I stood on a rock by the bank, washed my face, gargled, and prayed to the land called the castle on the other bank... Heavens! I bowed to the heavens with my heart, and my eyes filled with tears. The clear water ran ceaselessly, taking in its partners to the sea. I salute you!"[3] The New Village at Kijo covered an area of 2.5 hectares.[4] The population in 1918 was 18; 29 in 1919; 34 in 1920; 19 in 1921; 17 in 1922; and 11 in 1923.[5] At its first establishment, the Village

---

[3]. Mushakoji Saneatsu, *The Land* (Tokyo: Aranosha, 1921). This is a documentary work where Mushakoji records the search for and purchase of land in Kijo. Aranosha is a New Village publishing division established in 1920 in former Kitatoshima district in Tokyo prefecture.

[4]. *The Complete Works of Mushakoji Saneatsu,* vol. 4 (Tokyo: Shogakukan, 1988). Quoted in Liu Lishan, p. 202. According to Japanese measurement, 1 *cho* is 10 *tan*, 1 *tan* is 10 *se*, 1 *se* is 30 *tsubo*, 1 *tsubo* is 2 *jo*, 1 *jo* is 5 *go*, 1 *go* is 10 *shaku*, and 1 *shaku* is about 0.0331 square meters. 2 *cho*, 5 *tan* and 3 *se* total is 25,122.9 square meters, which translates into 2.51229 hectares.

[5]. Ibid.

required all members to participate in manual labor during an eight-hour workday. It had very loose acceptance criteria for its members. As long as they recognized the spirit of New Village, they could join regardless of origin, wealth, or status—so it quickly became a refuge for the marginalized: Koreans, leprosy patients, and other outcasts of society. In 1920, Mushakoji published an article sympathetic to the Korean independence movement in *The Dong-a Ilbo,* a Korean publication. He apologized for the "arrogance" of the Japanese and hoped that the Koreans would respond to the "barbaric Japanese" not with violence but with "peace, love, and justice," just as the Nazarenes responded to the oppression of the Romans by saving the Romans. Under the influence of this article, New Village accepted two Koreans as members in 1921.[6] The concept and organization of the New Village were reflected in two documents proposed in its beginning:

---

6. Tessa Morris-Suzuki, "Beyond Utopia: New Villages and Living Politics in Modern Japan and across Frontiers," in *History Workshop Journal* 85 (Oxford University Press, 2018), 47-71.

The Spirit of New Village

1. Our ideal is that all the world's peoples can fulfill their destinies, and each person can also grow fully.
2. Do not harm others just so you can exist.
3. You must set your life on the right path. Do not harm others' destinies and legitimate needs because of your own pleasures, joys, and freedom.
4. We must try our best that humankind across the world can share in the same spirit and the same way of life as us, so that all humankind can fulfill its obligations, enjoy freedom, and have decent lives that accomplish their destinies (including individuality).
5. Whoever wants to live in this way, and believes that it is possible to live in this way, and hopes that people all over the world can live in this way—these people are members of New Village and are our brothers and sisters.
6. We do not want conflict between countries and between classes. Those who enter New Village lead decent lives, work together, and

believe that the world we hope for will emerge, and we work hard for this.[7]

New Village Rules

1. The New Village was established in order to live in accordance with the spirit mentioned above. Where there is a proper method, it should be followed. We hope to abolish the rules in the future.
2. Those who are in agreement with the Spirit of New Village and participate are our members.
3. There are two kinds of members: first, those who practice according to the Spirit; second, those who agree with the Spirit but aren't in a position where they practice.
4. There are limitations on the first type of member; as for the second type, anyone can join.
5. The first type of member should complete voluntary labor at will. However, an exception

---

[7] "The Spirit of the New Village" has remained unchanged since it was written. I reference Sun Baigang's translation here; see *The New Village*, pp. 137-138.

shall be made for those who are ill, or where there are unavoidable events, and this must be agreed to by all.

6. Member comrades shall not order each other around.

7. Property owned by members of the first category is unconditionally given to New Village. However, within the first year after joining, they can still choose what to do with their assets. Afterwards, all assets will be donated unconditionally to New Village.

8. Each member shall be responsible for their own words and deeds.

9. Any person who is not in accordance with the Spirit, or unenthusiastic, may be ordered to leave. However, the decision shall be made after discussion with all members.

10. Volunteer labor and other village matters shall be decided by all. However, within the limits of not violating the Spirit, you need not agree.

11. The second type of member shall try their best to promote the Spirit of New Village to the masses, assist the village in its work, and complete that work. Those who have the ability

to pay membership dues shall donate over 50 yen per month at will.[8]

These two documents can be said to be the crystallization of Mushakoji's and his comrades' thought in founding New Village, the exploration of personal and social paths through the fog of the First World War. Although he was born an aristocrat, his conscience was captured by the inequality brought about by class differences. His sympathy for the masses who "worked for bread" led him to reflect on the deformation of labor caused by the rapid capitalist development in Japan from the Meiji to the Taisho era. His criticism of belligerent Japan proved that he could not accept the killings of the World War—and he even opposed socialist revolution in Russia because of its violence. In order to reconcile social contradictions and avoid violent revolution, he walked a third road beyond capitalism and socialism. He supported collective ownership of property, but opposed class struggle; believed

---

[8]. This is the 1920 revision of the "New Village Rules." See Sun Baigang, pp. 139-140. The membership fee mentioned in Article 11 was in Japanese yen at that time.

in freedom, but did not accept competition; he advocated for necessary labor, but paid attention to people's leisure; he pursued anarchist egalitarianism, mutual aid, and cooperation, but abandoned any associated violence. He emphasized personal will and opposed oppression; with the ideal of humans across the world following their destinies, he resisted nationalism and ethnocentrism.

These ideals were reflected in the two-level membership system, a far-sighted design for a progressive social experiment, which not only ensured the integrity of New Village's experimental base in the wilderness, but also gathered the strength of outside aid at the broader social level by lowering the threshold of belonging. It not only mobilized members outside the village to promote it, but also alleviated their moral anxieties for not being able to leave the "old world." Later evidence also proved that the life-sustaining nourishment in the form of financial and other resources provided by members outside the village was crucial to New Village.

The bedrock ideals of New Village can be found in its holidays. According to a letter Mushakoji wrote in the journal *New Village*, New Village has five rest days each month, and there are five festivals in the year—New Year's Day (January 1), Shakyamuni's birthday (April 8), Tolstoy's birthday (August 28), Rodin's birthday (November 14, also the founding day of New Village), and Jesus' birthday (December 25, Christmas).[9] Shakyamuni's compassion for all living beings, Jesus' salvation for all, Tolstoy's pan-laborism, and Rodin's belief in beauty were the ideological resources that Mushakoji had always drawn from.[10] However, his admiration of Tolstoy had modulated long before he began the New Village experiment. After all, Tolstoy's "extreme altruism," excessive emphasis on physical labor and excessive exclusion of mental labor seemed difficult to achieve in reality—so he introduced the "static theory of self," from the Belgian writer Maurice Maeterlinck, in order to find the most suitable position between

---

[9] See correspondence of December 7, 1918, by Mushakoji Saneatsu, *New Village*, vol. 2, no. 1, January 1919. Translated by Zhou Zuoren and included in his article "Japan's New Village," published in *New Youth*, vol. 6, no. 3, April 1919. See Zhou Zuoren, *Art and Life*, p. 233. However, the birth dates of Tolstoy and Rodin are incorrect; according to Wikipedia, Tolstoy was born on September 9, 1828, and Rodin on November 12, 1840.

[10] He wrote *Biography of Jesus* (New Village Publishing, 1920), *Biography of Buddha* (Kodansha, 1934), and *Biography of Tolstoy* (Saikensha, 1959).

"self-sacrifice" and "reasonable self-interest:" "He (Maeterlinck) taught me: we should focus on our own strengths, and improve our own strengths. The concept of 'ourselves' is profound, and difficult to comprehend."[11]

In July 1919, Zhou Zuoren visited Mushakoji, his wife Takeo Fusako, and their adopted daughter, Kikuko (the daughter of Kadenokoji Yasuko and her ex-husband, who later lived with Shiga Naoya and her mother), and three others who lived in the house across the river from the "lower castle." It, and the New Village main house and workshop in the "middle castle," were completed two months before. The main house was the dormitory for male members, including three 10-mat bedrooms, and was also the place where members gathered, with a library and canteen. The dormitories for female members were being built, so they were temporarily living on the upper level of the stables. The "upper castle" was where they worked: "It's all dry land, for planting some beans, wheat, corn, eggplant, sweet potato and

---

11. Mushakoji Saneatsu, "For Oneself and Others," *Shirakaba* (1912, no. 2). Cited in Liu Lishan, p. 134.

so on."[12] New Village had a mare, three goats, two pigs, two dogs, and a variety of chickens. However, the production of eggs was not enough for their own use, and they needed to purchase eggs from other local producers. The Village struggled, but failed, to be self-sufficient. For monthly living expenses, they needed at least 250 yen, and still depended on the membership dues donated by the local branches. The large expenses such as land purchases, material transportation, housing construction, agricultural tools, water conservancy, and so on, depended on Mushakoji's remuneration (he was preparing to sell his Abiko residence at that time). Zhou Zuoren, as a Chinese subscriber and advocate for the White Birch Society and *Shirakaba*, was treated with courtesy, but was also asked to work in the field—helping him experience the spirit of "cooperation through farming, sharing pain and joy" of the New Village. He felt "great joy and honor."[13] His article "A Visit to New Village in Japan," records his experiences there in great detail, depicting an image of the

---

[12] Zhou Zuoren, "A Visit to a New Village in Japan," *Art and Life*, pp. 249-255.

[13] Ibid.

Japanese "utopia" as making stumbling progress for a Chinese audience who was experiencing the process of the May 4th New Culture Movement.

At the Mushakoji Saneatsu Memorial Museum in Chofu, I watched a 16 mm black and white silent film that lasted 7 minutes 24 seconds. It was filmed in 1922 by Mushakoji's junior classman at Peers School, Yukio Akimiti. It recorded the daily life of New Village at Kijo and the fourth anniversary celebration held on November 14. On the rapids of Omaru River, someone was ferrying in. The members on the shore stood by the rocks and waved. Some were playing in the water. Beyond the river were the farmlands owned by local people, and the ancient mountains surrounding the secret world of New Village. When the bell rang in the morning, the members filed into the canteen. After breakfast, they gathered around the canteen to see the work assignments for the day. Men ploughed, threshed, tended vegetables, built houses, loaded firewood, and read and wrote; women washed clothes in the river, and sewed inside their houses. Mushakoji weeded his vegetable patch and greeted guests at his door. The grass was verdant, and the distant mountain was silent. For rest, they could either take a walk in the woods or go boating on the river. On the anniversary, children played games and adults wore costumes and held parades. They dressed up as tribal chiefs and as Chaplin, and danced in circles...[14]

Although the film presented an idyllic image of rustic work and life—a free, unfettered paradise—all utopias face problems when they are practiced. New Village was no different, contending with both internal conflict and external difficulty. Kimura Syouta was one of the first people to criticize the New Village initiative. A writer and translator, he and his wife followed Mushakoji to Kijo as some of the first members of the village. New Village stipulates that all members should hand over their personal property to the collective for overall distribution, and that the collective should be responsible for any expenses for living, eating, medical treatment, and travel during ordinary times. Each person would receive a monthly allowance of one yen (half-yen

---

14. Yukio Akimiti, *New Village at Hyuga*, 16mm film, original copy, Mushakoji Saneatsu Memorial Museum in Chofu, data number: V-5031. This film has been digitized and is available on the official website (www.saneatsu.org), but for copyright reasons can only be accessed at the museum.

for children). Takeo Fusako was responsible for the financial allocations, but her arrangements were often considered unfair—because she was perceived to give more money to those she was friendly with, or partial to. Kimura Syouta was not only dissatisfied with Takeo, but was also critical of Mushakoji. Although Mushakoji was a member of New Village, he had not put his other career aside. He often went back and forth to Tokyo, continuing to participate in the literary and artistic activities of the White Birch Society and spending less time doing labor in the village than the others—instead, he mainly sat writing at the desk. Kimura Syouta believed that, during this early period for New Village, everyone should become familiar with agricultural affairs as quickly as possible, promote production, and help achieve economic independence. For this reason, he even suggested suspending the distribution of allowances to invest as much money as possible into the construction of New Village—thus, he belonged to what became known as the "labor faction." Mushakoji believed that his writing and activities in Tokyo could increase income from royalties in order to contribute to New Village. He insisted on the allowance system and advocated that there should be more leisure and artistic activity in the village—he belonged to the "art faction." The two factions argued bitterly. In the end, Kimura Syouta left New Village disappointed, in May 1919. The *Osaka Daily News*, which had paid attention to New Village since its beginning, reported that a "terrible internal collapse" had occurred.[15]

In addition, even if New Village was founded in the mountains and the wilderness, it could not escape the constraints of the wider society and government rule. Local farmers regarded these idealists from the big cities as rich, and raised the price of eggs and grain accordingly. When they intended to buy more land, the village head at Ishikawauchi quoted them a price that was several times higher than the market rate.[16] Plainclothes and military police also went to New Village once a month to monitor their movement and thought. In 1921, one member of New Village, Yokoi Kunisaburou, was conscripted. Subsequently, Miyazaki Prefecture built an army airport and also stationed troops near New Village.

---

15. See Liu Lishan, p. 210.
16. See Zhou Zuoren, *Art and Life*, p. 251.

Another member of New Village, Sugiyama Masao, was conscripted as forced labor.[17] For New Village, which was short of people and a stable workforce, this made matters much worse. The final relocation of New Village from Kijo was due to their inability to defy a Miyazaki reservoir plan that would use the Omaru River to generate hydroelectric power.

In terms of his personal life, the marriage between Mushakoji and Takeo changed in 1922. Takeo fell in love with Sugiyama Masao, who was ten years younger than she. Mushakoji divorced her and married Meshigawa Yasuko, who had entered the village the year before. Later on, Takeo was regarded as an early feminist in Japan. She had been married to Mushakoji for ten years, and "didn't understand true love until she entered the village."[18] Her extramarital affair with Sugiyama, though deeply painful to Mushakoji, also transformed his idea of womanhood. In an article from 1928, "Three Random Writings," he wrote: "Chastity cannot be used as a yardstick

---

17. See Liu Lishan, p. 207.
18. "Mushakoji Fusako," *Rediscovering Home: 101 People in Miyazaki,* ed. Miyazaki Prefecture, (Nichi Nichi Shimbun, 1999). https://www.pref.miyazaki.lg.jp/contents/org/chiiki/seikatu/ miyazaki101/hito/062/062.html

to judge women... Even many shortcomings do not mean that someone is rotten."[19] Takeo and Sugiyama did not formally marry until 1932. After New Village moved to Moroyama, the two continued living at Kijo until Sugiyama died in 1983, and Takeo died in 1989. They truly lived up to the pledge that "members should live permanently at New Village." Mushakoji, regardless of their past, agreed that Takeo could keep his family name, and voiced support for the couple's life together. When Takeo was interviewed in her old age, she recalled that she "was deeply pained, was disillusioned, and there was a residual pride formed by my early life of abundance. Fortunately, with the warm support of Sugiyama, I was able to survive this period of mental and physical suffering."[20] The marriage of Mushakoji and Meshigawa resulted in the birth of a daughter, Shinko, and then another, Taeko, in New Village. In December 1925, because of the gap between the ideal and the reality, and in order to take care of his sick mother, Mushakoji left New Village with his wife, daughter, and Kikuko.

---

19. Published in the November 1928 issue of *The Great Harmony*. Translation in Liu Lishan, p. 236.
20. "Mushakoji Fusako," in *Rediscovering Home: 101 People in Miyazaki*.

By that time, Shiga Naoya had moved to Nara, so Mushakoji also took his mother from Tokyo to Nara, where he set up a new household and became a close neighbor of Shiga's. Mushakoji's departure from the village did not mean that he gave up on New Village. In his later career, he continued to contribute to it as an outside member, and worked hard to support its future development.

According to statistics from the 1973 article, "The Current Situation in New Village," if the money that Mushakoji devoted to the cause of New Village throughout his life was converted into yen of that year, it would reach 100 million yen.[21] In the early days of the establishment of New Village at Kijo, his colleagues in the White Birch Society, Shiga Naoya, Yanagi Soetsu and Kishida Ryusei, also donated generously. Yanagi Soetsu and Nagayo Yoshiro each visited, in 1920 and 1921. In order to prepare for the construction of the White Birch Art Museum, Mushakoji successfully persuaded the Osaka industrialist Yamamoto Koyata to buy Van Gogh's *Sunflowers*, and brought it to

---

21. Watanabe Kanji, "The Present State of New Village," in Liu Lishan, p. 212.

Japan for exhibition in 1919. In 1920, he also asked Yamamoto to purchase a piece of land for him in Kayane, Kawaminami, near Kijo—for the second New Village.[22] In the same year he also established Aranosha in Tokyo as the publishing arm of New Village. The 1923 Great Kanto Earthquake greatly reduced the assistance of outside members. By 1924, however, after years of promotional material, activities, speeches and lobbying, in addition to the headquarters at Kijo, the second New Village at Kawaminami (land only; no members ever lived there), and the publishing wing in Tokyo, New Villages could be found in Tokyo, Osaka, Kyoto, Kobe, Nagano, Hamamatsu, Hakodate, Aomori, Yokohama, Fukuoka, Kure, Gifu, Akita, Yamaguchi, Saiki, Otaru, Okayama, Niigata, Miyazaki, Hiroshima, Koromo, and Beijing and Dalian, in China.[23] There were now 23 branches, and, by 1929, 800 outside members.[24]

---

22. Mushakoji Saneatsu Memorial Museum, *100 Years of New Village: 1918-2018*, p. 18.
23. "The Location of New Village and its Branches," in *The New Village*, trans. Sun Baigang, pp. 141-143.
24. *The Complete Works of Mushakoji Saneatsu,* vol. 4 (Tokyo: Shogakukan, 1988). In Liu Lishan, p. 214.

The posts of the New Village Life and Culture Museum
and the New Village Art Museum, Moroyama.
Photo by Ou Ning, 2019.

NEW VILLAGE DEBATE

When Mushakoji first proposed the New Village initiative in May 1918, it immediately caused a stir, with many Japanese intellectuals responding. This "New Village Debate" continued through 1923. The first person who responded was Sakai Toshihiko, the first person to introduce utopian literature from the West to Japan, and the socialist colleague of Kotoku Shusui, with whom he co-founded the *Heiminsha* (Commoners Society) and co-translated *The Communist Manifesto*. Sakai published "A Critique of New Village" in the June 1918 issue of *Central Review*. Following that, another socialist, Yamakawa Hitoshi, published "The Ideal Village for an Artist" in the July 1918 issue of *Shin Nihon* (*New Japan*). Another member of the White Birch Society, Arishima Takeo, was following Sakai closely and published "To Mushakoji" in the July issue of *Central Review*. Anarchist Osugi Sakae published "The Affairs of Mushakoji Saneatsu and New Village" in the May, 1922 issue of *Shincho* (*New Tide*). A student of Mushakoji's, Kaneko Yobun, who had co-founded *Tane maku Hito* (*The Sower*, a Japanese proletarian literary magazine in the early 1920s) with Omi Komaki, published the book *The Life of Mushakoji Saneatsu* in October 1922, which also commented on New Village. Some of these intellectuals with a socialist or anarchist bent described New Village as an escape from Realpolitik, and others predicted that it would fail.[1]

These people, like Mushakoji, actually aspired to a communist-like utopia, but each had their own ways and paths for achieving it. The socialist movement in Japan experienced a cold winter period after the High Treason Incident. After entering the

---

[1] Other antagonists in the New Village Dispute include Honma Hisao, Eguchi Kiyoshi, Kawakami Hajime, Kato Kazuo, Hirabayashi Hatsunosuke, and Takata Yasuma.

Taisho era, the Russian revolution encouraged them, the Rice Riots gave them training in street struggle, and there was a rise in civil rights movements. The "eternal rule by Mikado" was under attack, and the constitutional movement of Inukai Tsuyoshi against the "six elders," like Yamagata Aritomo, and other events, gave them hope for parliamentary politics. So moderates like Sakai Toshihiko, Yamakawa Hitoshi, and Arahata Kanson joined the Japanese Communist Party, founded in 1922, while radicals like Osugi Sakai advocated violent revolution. Later, because of disappointment with the Soviet regime and the Communist International, he chose anarchism. In his early years, Kaneko Yobun followed Mushakoji to Abiko, but later became a leftist writer. Although he did not join any party, he was still considered "a soldier of the proletarian literary revolution." Undoubtedly, they all regarded Mushakoji's New Village experiment as an individual artist returning to the countryside to find an idyllic semi-agricultural life, so as to stay far from domestic affairs and class struggle. Even if Mushakoji had the desire to carry out social improvements through New Village, "an oasis in a desert does not turn the desert into fertile soil even if it exists for tens of thousands of years."[2] This kind of social improvement was no different from the projects of Robert Owen and Charles Fourier in the 19th century. Friedrich Engels called this utopian socialism rather than scientific socialism, which is engaged in "realistic" struggle.

Arishima Takeo even more bluntly stated that New Village "will ultimately end in failure." He had paid tribute to Mushakoji as a literary and artistic figure who chose "to be a reformer rather than a eulogist" during this "era of transformation," but, "your New Village is surrounded by capitalism, which is still exerting its frenzy of power... Even if the people living in your New Village have some awareness of this, as soon as they encounter something out of the ordinary, it will only lead to disappointment."[3] This made Mushakoji very angry, and the two of them had a temporary falling out. Nevertheless, the respect Arishima had for New Village was sincere. In 1922, out of his own belief in communism, he made an astonishing move, transferring a total of 459 acres of land he inherited

---

[2] Yamakawa Hitoshi, "The Ideal Village for an Artist."
[3] Liu Lishan, p. 206.

from his deceased father, Arishima Takeshi, to its 70 tenants for free, turning it into a collectively owned "symbiotic farm."[4]

The Arishima family farm was located in Hokkaido, in the town of Kaributo (now known as Niseko), in Iburinokuni. Arishima Takeshi received it from the local government in 1900 and 1914, with the Hokkaido State-Owned Uncultivated Land Treatment Law, which encouraged land reclamation. He invested huge sums of money to recruit tenants for farming and management, and later it became an important source of wealth for the family. After graduating from Peers School, Arishima Takeo enrolled in Sapporo Agricultural College for the purpose of managing the Kaributo Farm in the future. However, his interests changed later on, and he went to Harvard University to study for a Master of Arts degree. After returning home, he became an important representative writer of the White Birch Society. In 1922, the national organization, the Levelers Association, (later renamed the Buraku

---

[4] The farm was originally intended to be called the Together Farm, but later it was decided that it would be called the Collective Farm. It was finally decided to be called Symbiotic Farm.

Liberation League), which was dedicated to the causes of fighting segregation, fighting poverty, and seeking liberation, was founded. There was a wave of "liberation" happening in Japanese society at the time, and Arishima began to have writer's block, so he simply announced that he was temporarily putting his pen aside. On July 17, two days after the founding of the Japanese Communist Party, he went to Kaributo Farm to gather all its tenants together, and announced his surprising decision:

"As the basic natural components of production, things such as air, water, and land should be jointly used by the entire human race, and the results of their use must be beneficial to the entire human race and must not be privately owned solely for the benefit of an individual. However, in today's world, most usable land is occupied by individuals. Such a phenomenon generates events that greatly harm humanity, and these have become ubiquitous. In view of this, I hope that this farm will from here on be collectively owned by all of you. Together you will share responsibility for the land, assist each other, and strive to produce."[5] The reasons given by him for this speech, explained in a later work "Farewell to My Tenants," also known as "The Declaration of Farm Liberation," are completely consistent with Kropotkin's assertion in the first chapter of *The Conquest of Bread*, "Our Riches," that "all belongs to all, all things are for all men."[6]

Common sense dictates that the material wealth produced and accumulated by humans through continuous technological improvement over thousands of years of history has produced abundance—so why are there still so many poor people? The real situation that Arishima saw in rural Hokkaido resulted in an intuitive conclusion. The farmers there lived in dilapidated thatched cottages, and struggled to make ends meet. In addition, with half a year of snow, they could not simply spend their days "hibernating," but went to earn money by clearing snow on railways and fishing for herring. If you had some money, you could drink to ward off the cold. If you drank

---

5. Arishima Takeo, "Farewell to My Tenants," *Spring*, October 1922. Translated by Liu Lishan, appendix to *Japanese White Birch School Writers and Chinese Writers*, pp. 599-600.
6. Peter Kropotkin, *The Conquest of Bread and Other Writings* (Cambridge: Cambridge University Press, 1995), p. 19.

alcohol, you also gambled. If you gambled, you would go into debt. If you went into debt, you would have to pre-sell your crops. Even in a good year, your income would already have been consumed in advance, so you would still fall into an abyss of poverty. The root of this cycle was private property, capitalism, and "treacherous businessmen"—and in the fact that farmers did not work on behalf of their own needs, but to produce goods for those few who could use those goods for trade and profit. As Arishima wrote: "The entirety of the capitalist system is a massive force, occupying thousands of years history, and with extraordinary power it has eroded the different areas of life: education, habits, and customs. On the contrary, unfortunately, the communist spirit and culture are weak among tenants. It can be said that, compared to the situation in the cities, the capitalist spirit is particularly rampant in rural areas."[7]

He made up his mind, and planned to live off money made from his literary work in the future—

---

[7] Arishima Takeo, "The Liberation of Kaributo Farm," *Otaru Shimbun*, May 20-21, 1923. See Liu Lishan, Appendix to *Japanese White Birch Writers and Chinese Writers*, p. 613.

while "liberating" the farm for tenants. But he was not optimistic about the future of the Kaributo Symbiotic Farm. And he was just as pessimistic about New Village: "The tenants on my farm are very different from the members of New Village. The members of New Village are relatively intelligent, they agree with the opinions of Mushakoji Saneatsu, and have purpose in putting beliefs and values to practical tests. However, the tenants on my farm are completely untrained and lack knowledge; even my intentions cannot be fully understood, making the future of the farm difficult to predict. The difference is that New Village relies on donations or other funds to maintain its livelihood. Relying solely on the production of New Village is not enough to survive."[8] Since the future was uncertain, why did Arishima insist on his actions? This can be attributed to his compassion and "unbearable" feelings: "I liberated the land, and my actions were not to win praise or respect from the world, or to appear as someone with lofty ideals, but to satisfy

---

8. Arishima Takeo, "From Private Farm to Collective Farm," *Liberation*, Vol. 5, No. 3, March 1923. Liu Lishan, Appendix to *Japanese White Birch Writers and Chinese Writers*, p. 604.

my own conscience. It was something I had to do."[9] Unfortunately, in the second year after he gave up his private farm, he also gave up his life and gave up the world.

Arishima was like Nekhlyudov in Tolstoy's *A Landowner's Morning*—an idealist who attempted to break through class divisions. Both he and Mushakoji were deeply influenced by Tolstoy. Tolstoy gave up his count status in 1884 and decided to work and live like other, ordinary people. In 1886, when he was almost 60 years old, he decided to walk back to his Yasnaya Polyana manor from his Moscow home on foot. The whole journey was more than 200 kilometers. On the way, he only slept on the floors of farmhouses, or crowded into small inns with other travelers. A photo at the time shows him leaning on a cane by the roadside, wearing a felt hat, a farmer's robe, and carrying a cloth bundle—like a beggar in a famine year. This image might have prompted Paul Johnson, the British historian, to satirize Tolstoy's "class transvestism."[10] But when the image

---

9. Arishima Takeo, "The Liberation of Kaributo Farm." See Liu Lishan, p. 614.
10. Paul Johnson, *Intellectuals: From Marx and Tolstoy to Sartre and Chomsky* (Harper Collins e-books), p. 127.

was spread everywhere through newspapers and magazines, people undoubtedly regarded this great aristocrat and great writer as a saint of asceticism. Arishima's Symbiotic Farm and Mushakoji's New Village both followed Tolstoy's actions to achieve class transformation. The transformation from the upper class to the lower class was of their own accord, so I think it may be more accurate to use Paulo Freire's term "class suicide"[11] to describe it. In the revolution initiated by the Communist Party of China, many young people from bourgeois families defected to Yan'an in late 1930s, and this was also "class suicide" inspired by revolutionary ideals.

The New Village Debate created an opportunity for Japanese intellectuals to openly discuss utopianism and the ideal society. In this regard, the commonalities among participants outweighed their differences. And apart from critics, there were many supporters—Yanagi Soetsu, Shiga Naoya, Nagayo Yoshiro—who all had close personal relations with Mushakoji. There were also the novelists Hirotsu Kazuo and Kikuchi Hiroshi. In the July 1918 issue of

---

11. Paulo Freire, *Pedagogy in Process: The Letters to Guinea-Bissau* (New York, Seabury Press, 1977), p. 16.

Central Review, there was a feature on "A Look at the People of the White Birch Society," which covered New Village as well. In addition to Arishima Takeo's "To Mushakoji," there was also an article by the novelist, poet, and Japanese translator of *The Complete Works of Lu Xun*, Sato Haruo, entitled "Thank You All." He thought that the White Birch Society pursued beauty, while New Village sought kindness. The latter was a further action, and regardless of its success or failure, was worth cheering on. Instead of joining New Village himself, he immersed himself in the literary world to explore utopianism. In 1919, he published the utopian work *Beautiful Town*, and in 1929 he published the dystopian work *Record of a Conspiracy*. Buddhist playwright Kurata Hyakuzo, who was an outside member of New Village, naturally expressed his support. In 1920, he published "About New Village" over three issues of *Gassho* magazine. Interestingly, he looked at New Village from a religious perspective, believing that it could be a place of spiritual refuge—avoiding donations from unclean sources, and being vigilant against the secular world.[12]

Kurata's suggestions came from his experience of having joined Nishida Tenko's salvation group Ittoen (One-Lamp Garden). When Nishida was young, he had been responsible for a land reclamation project in Hokkaido. The conflict between tenant farmers and landlords led him to decide to leave the farm and try "life without struggle." In 1904, he founded Ittoen in Shinomiyayanagiyama, a suburb of Kyoto, as a social experiment in purifying morality through community service and education. The members of Ittoen worshiped "light"—meaning gods, Buddhas, nature, and "nothingness." They relied on mendicant work for food and frequently visited homes, schools, and social institutions in Kyoto and around the country to clean toilets for people. In 1921, Nishida published the book *A Life of Repentance*, with a cover photo of him holding a broom. It became the symbol of Ittoen. Even today

---

[12] Nishiyama Taku, "Utopianism in the Thought and Action of Ishikawa Sanshiro: The Theory of the Ideal Society and Social Reform by the Intellectual in Modern Japan," Waseda University dissertation, Graduate School of Social Sciences, 2009. Waseda University Repository: https://waseda.repo.nii.ac.jp

Ittoen is still in operation. It is registered as a legal entity with over 200 members in Kyoto, carrying out agriculture, architecture, publishing, education, and other work. It holds several intellectual and moral training sessions every year and is the oldest surviving utopian organization in Japan.

In fact, Mushakoji mentions in his "Dialogue on New Village" that "although the people of New Village are different from monks, they could be considered kinds of monks. They are the monks of the new life."[13] However, although he revered Jesus and the Buddha, he was not actually a believer. If he could have converted the religious power of the Shakers, the Harmonites, and the Perfectionists of the 19th century into a secular form, then the utopian cause of New Village might have fared differently. Faced with the debate that he himself helped promote, and coupled with internal strife that occurred during the early days of New Village, Mushakoji grew irritable, and tired of constant confrontation. After several rounds of verbal battles, he withdrew, and gradually the New Village Debate subsided.

---

13. *The New Village*, trans. Sun Baigang, p. 49.

The bust memorial statue of Mushakoji Saneatsu in Saneatsu Park, Chofu.
Photo by Ou Ning, 2019.

ECHOES IN CHINA

After Zhou Zuoren published his article "Japan's New Village" in *New Youth* (No. 3, Volume 6, April 1919), introducing New Village to China, the news of latest developments of New Village continued to spread. Shortly after returning from a trip to New Village, at the invitation of Zhou Enlai, who was studying at Nankai University, Zhou Zuoren gave the speech "The Spirit of New Village" at the Tianjin Awareness Society. The speech was then published in *The Republican Daily News* in Shanghai on November 23, 1919, and in *New Youth* (Volume 7, No. 2) on January 1, 1920. In December of that year, Mao Zedong, who worked as a history teacher at Xiuye Primary School in Changsha, published an article entitled "The Work of the Students" in *Hunan Education Monthly*, which mentioned New Village. In January 1920, Hu Shih gave his speech, "A New Life without Individualism," in Tianjin, Tangshan, and other places, fiercely criticizing New Village as introduced by Zhou Zuoren. Zhou immediately defended New Village by writing in the *Morning Post* (Supplement) on January 24th, "Explaining the New Village Movement: In Response to Mr. Hu." Hu's speech was published in *The China Times* the next day, and reprinted in the March issue of *The Renaissance* (Volume 2, No. 3). Zhou also delivered a speech on "The Ideal and the Reality of New Village" at the Beijing Social Progress Association on June 19, and published the speech in the *Morning Post* on the 23rd. For a while after the May Fourth Movement, "New Village" was a term that popped up everywhere in China, and Japan's New Village Debate even touched China's intelligentsia.

The "new life without individualism" advocated by Hu supported "true individualism"—meaning independent thinking, adherence to truth, fearlessness toward authority, and disregard for personal gain. At the same time, it was also a negation of "false individualism"—selfish egoism and "personal individualism." His criticism of New Village as promoted by Zhou was similar to criticisms by Japanese socialists and anarchists: "The recent new village movement, like utopian agriculturalism in France and America in the 19th century, or the Japanese New Village Movement, is, in my opinion, fundamentally the same as a reclusive life in the mountains." This was a "retreat," and a "concession" rather than a "struggle." Moreover, the "pan-laborism" advocated by New Village fundamentally negated the social division of labor as well as human evolution. Hu disagreed most of all with Zhou's statement that "transforming society starts with transforming individuals." On the contrary, he believed that "individuals are made by countless forces in society. Transforming society starts with transforming the various forces that create society as well as individuals. Transforming society is transforming individuals."[1] This was in

---

1. Hu Shih, "A New Life without Individualism," *Collected Essays of Hu Shih*, vol. 4, book 1 (Beijing: Capital Economic and Trade University Press, 2013), pp. 452-458.

line with Osugi Sakae's criticism of Mushakoji who didn't engage in class struggle and didn't advocate overthrowing the existing system but hoped to gradually achieve social improvements through personal cultivation. The only difference was that Osugi Sakae's criticism was more radical.

Zhou naturally did not agree that New Village was "personalist." He defended it saying, "In the eyes of most people, the 'humane life' they advocate could not be achieved without violence. But they believe that it can be achieved using peaceful means, so they just go ahead and do it."[2] Zhou believed that in order to transform society without violent revolution, we could only start from the individual. Hu's rebuke made Sun Baigang, Yu Dafu's classmate studying in Japan, angry even several years later. When he translated and published Mushakoji's *New Village* in 1926, he also wrote a translator's preface that refuted Hu: "Turning the pages of history, it is nothing more than individuals creating society, society creating individuals, individuals rebuilding society, society rebuilding individuals, and mutual

---

[2] Zhou Zuoren, "Explaining the New Village Movement: In Response to Mr. Hu," in Chen Zishan and Zhang Tierong eds., *Zhou Zuoren Uncollected Works,* book 1 (Haikou: Hainan International Press and Publication Center, 1995), pp. 318-320.

transformations." He believed that "individuals and society are mutually causal." Both Hu and Zhou made the mistake of separating society and individuals. Sun Baigang's advocacy of New Village was much more powerful than Zhou's because it understood both the society and the individual as equally important.

Hu's accusations were indeed a headache for supporters of Mushakoji's New Village. In his speech, he passionately exclaimed: "Good boys and girls! There are so many things we can do for our old village! How many opium lamps does it have? How many people are killed by morphine needles there? How many women bind their feet in the village? What is school like in the village? How much money did the gentlemen in the village make selling the election ballots this year? How is the temple still so prosperous? How many lives were ended by doctors in the village? Did you know that the coal miners in the village only get five coppers a day? Do you know how many female workers in the village are forced into prostitution by poverty? The factory in the village doesn't have fire escapes. And yesterday a fire broke out, killing over a hundred people. Did you know that? The child-wife bought for a child-husband had her leg broken by her mother-in-law. A gentleman in the village starved his daughter to death to retain her virtue. Did you know about that?" In such a "filthy old village," "What right do we have to abandon all these things we need to do and live in some secluded new village?" Hu cited the Social Settlements movement that had emerged in Europe and America at the time as an example, reminding young people "not to follow the solitary life," but encouraging them to use their "non-individualistic new life" to "transform the old society into a new society, and old villages into new villages"—which was different from what Zhou had said about using violence.[3] I don't know if Y. C. James Yen, who had returned from Princeton University that summer after completing his master's degree, read this speech or not. But perhaps it was what led him to launch his campaign of mass education and rural reconstruction in China at the time, which was surprisingly consistent with Hu's suggestions.

In the Chinese context of the May 4th New

---

[3] All above quoted from Hu Shih, "A New Life without Individualism."

Culture Movement, the term "new village" not only referred to the actual New Village, but expanded into a synonym for communitarian utopias that "avoided the world," as well as experiments in social transformation that "joined the world." Li Dazhao, who was interested in communist ideas, may have seen Friedrich Engels' 1845 essay, "Description of Recently Founded Communist Colonies Still in Existence." He collected utopian materials from the 19th century, and wrote the essay "The Religious New Village Movement in America" in *Weekly Review* (No. 31, "New Year's Issue," January 1920). Later, after Qu Qiubai's enthusiastic response and urging, he wrote "A Brief Biography of Robert Owen and His New Village Movement" in the fourth issue of the semi-monthly *Criticism* ("New Village Issue," December 8). According to his plan, he intended to introduce four types of "new villages" to China: "(1) religious new villages, (2) Owenite new villages, (3) Fourierist new villages, (4) Icanrian Communities." However, in the end, he only wrote about the first two, and there was no time for the latter two to be introduced. His religious new villages included the Ephrata Community, the Society of Shakers, the Harmony Society, the Zoar Village, the Amana Society, the Bethel and Arora Colonies, and the Oneida Community. He also wrote about Owen's New Lanark (New Harmony was not discussed). These utopian experiments of the pre-Marxist era opened up a broader perspective for the interests of Chinese intellectuals aroused by the Japanese New Village movement.[4]

In the spring of 1920, Wang Gongbi, who did his graduate studies at Waseda University, returned to his hometown of Xiaowuying Village, Xihua County, Henan Province (today's Qingnian Town, Shaoling District, Luohe City). When he was in Japan, he met Mushakoji and maintained contact after returning home, often receiving the magazine *New Village* from him. After a thorough investigation of Xiaowuying Village, he formed the Essence Group with his tenant Zhang Tiesheng, his clan member Wang Shuyi, and Henan Senior Normal School graduates Zhu Ruiting and Ge Fei as the core leadership. They mobilized

---

[4]. These two articles were included in China Li Dazhao Research Association ed., *The Complete Works of Li Dazhao,* Volume III (Beijing: People's Publishing House, 2006): "The Religious New Village Movement in America," pp. 151-163; and "Biography of Robert Owen and His New Village Movement," pp. 245-251.

around 1,500 people in his village and neighboring ones to establish the Youth Autonomous Society, organize a self-defense corps, elect candidates for village office and a mediation committee through election, and announced that Xiaowuying Village would change its name to Qingnian Village (Youth Village). Their plan was to make Qingnian Village into a "new village" where "everyone will participate in labor, every family will have land to farm on, rich and poor alike will have food to eat, and men and women will share power equally."[5] In October of that year, Wang Gongbi donated his family's land, houses, and library, gave up his salary, and established a public school and experimental farm inside the village. He emphasized the "integration of agriculture and education" in order to develop methods of both learning and sustenance with the villagers. He did not gather his colleagues from the city and then move to the countryside to establish his own community, as did Mushakoji. Instead, he directly entered the locale of his hometown to conduct these

---

[5] See *The Chronological Biography of Wang Gongbi* (self-published manuscript, 1970); and Wang Jinyu and Dou Kewu, "Comments on Wang Gongbi's Life in New Village," *Journal of Zhengzhou University (Philosophy and Social Sciences Edition)*, 1987, no. 4, pp. 51-56.

experiments. It lasted until 1926, attracting many rural reconstruction groups in China at the time to visit, including the National Association of the Mass Education Movements (MEM) in Ding Xian led by Y. C. James Yen, and the Xiaozhuang Normal School in Nanjing led by Tao Xingzhi. Wang Gongbi's "new village" experiment came to an end due to the rampant banditry in Henan Province at that time (Qingnian Village was destroyed and looted by Yuan Ying's thousand-person bandit brigade in October 1926). In response to the banditry in Henan, Peng Yuting and Bie Tingfang launched the more powerful Wanxi Self-Governance Movement in 1927.

Although the New Village doctrine of Mushakoji was widely known throughout China, it could not be replicated realistically with the conditions on the ground at that time. Li Dazhao had introduced the communitarian utopias of the 19th century, and he himself soon turned to Marxist class struggle. In February 1920, Zhou Zuoren established the Beijing branch of Japan's New Village at his own home. It was really only a gesture of support to Mushakoji and was not practical at all. One week after *New Youth* published an announcement of the establishment of the New Village in Beijing on April 1, on April 7, Mao Zedong visited Zhou Zuoren at his Badaowan Hutong address listed in *New Youth*. The purpose of his visit to Zhou Zuoren is still unknown, but in fact, while an assistant at the library of Peking University a year before, he had already learned of New Village. After returning to Changsha from Beijing in 1919, he had "a proposal to build a New Village at Mount Yuelu," in which the first step would be to "start a school which will apply an educational doctrine based on the principles of social thought." His proposal, "The Work of the Students" was published in *Hunan Education Monthly*:

"To create new schools and to practice new education must be closely connected with creating new families and a new society. The main theme of the new education is to create a new life. ...Each and every student in the new schools will be a member of the new family he creates. As the number of students in the new schools gradually increases, the number of new families created will also gradually increase. Several new families joining together can create a new society. There are so many kinds of new societies that I cannot name them all. To mention some notable examples, there are: public childcare centers, public nursing homes, public schools, public libraries, public banks, public farms, public factories, public consumers' associations, public theatres, public hospitals, public parks, museums, and autonomous associations. The combination of such new schools and new societies will give rise to a 'new village.' I consider the area around Mount Yuelu to be the most suitable location near Changsha for establishing such a new village." He believed that according to the world trends at the time, his plan would have supporters: "In order to spread their socialism, many Russian youth have gone to the villages to live among the peasants. Among Japanese youth, there has recently flourished a so-called 'New Village Movement.' The United States of America and one of its colonies, the Philippines, also have popular 'work-study programs.' Our students studying abroad have also followed suit: They have formed the 'Work-Study Club' in America, and the 'Work-Study Association' in France. Therefore, if we are truly sincere about creating a new life, we should not be afraid that we will not have supporters."[6]

However, because of his busy participation in the Hunan Autonomy Movement, and the expulsion of Zhang Jingyao (the military governor of Hunan province from 1918 to 1920), Mao Zedong's plan was a dead letter. He put aside his utopian dream, and began to organize the Socialist youth corps and Communist groups in Changsha. In 1921, he went to Shanghai to participate in the founding of the Communist Party of China (CPC), and then embarked on the road of Realpolitik with party struggle. It was not until he founded New China and gained supreme leadership that his dream of a "new village" was realized through the People's Communes, in 1958.

Practically speaking, the New Village doctrine was inevitably reversed by reality after its introduction to China. Like the "world trends" that surged in the fervent mind of young Mao Zedong, it can be seen that various new ideological trends in

---

6. Mao Zedong, "The Work of the Students," *Hunan Education Monthly*, volume 1, no. 2, December 1, 1919. The English version cited from Stuart Schram ed., John King Fairbank Center tr., *Mao's Road to Power: Revolutionary Writings, 1912-49, Volume I: Pre-Marxist Period, 1912-1920* (New York: M.E. Sharpe, 1992), p.450, pp.454-455.

China at that time were truly surging. In that time, of the early republic and its political chaos, each person was striving to explore future directions, and hoping to find China's unique path. Wang Gongbi used the reality of China to transform Mushakoji's New Village doctrine into a rural autonomy movement, while the work-study groups of students from various regions transformed it into an experiment of half-work, half-study communities in the cities.

In the summer of 1919, the news of Li Chao—a student at Peking National Women's Normal School—shocked public opinion when she broke off relations with her family and walked out like Nora in Henrik Ibsen's *A Doll's House*. With tuberculosis and without the money for treatment, she died without any family members at her side. Seeing this, Wang Guangqi, the founder of the Young China Association, published the article "A New Life in the City" in the *Morning Post* on December 4 of the same year, proposing to establish a "work-study mutual aid group" in Beijing to provide economic security for poor students who pursued emancipation. He suggested that members of this group should "work six hours a day and study three." The income obtained from joint work would be jointly owned by the group. The necessary clothing, food, and housing of members would be provided by the group; the education, medical, and book expenses required by members would also be provided by the group.[7] In January 1920, with the support of Cai Yuanpei, Chen Duxiu, Li Dazhao, Hu Shih, Zhou Zuoren, and other big names in education, the Beijing Work-Study Mutual Aid Group successfully raised funds through *New Youth*, *The Journal of the Young China Association,* and other publications, and quickly used them toward their experiment. After becoming members of the group, students declared their separation from family, marriage, and school, and implemented a communal system. Within three months, Chen Zhidu in Tianjin, Hui Daiying in Wuhan, and 26 other people in Shanghai, including Chen Duxiu, Wang Guangqi, Zuo Shunsheng, Kang Baiqing, Zhang Guotao, Mao Zedong, Peng Huang, and Zong Baihua, launched work-study mutual aid groups. Nanjing, Guangzhou, Yangzhou, and other places also responded to the call. However, all these groups existed for only a

---

7. Zhao Hong, *The Chinese Dream of a New Village* (Guiyang: Guizhou People's Publishing House, 2014) p. 82.

short time. By the beginning of 1921 they all had more or less dissolved, many of them joining the newly established CPC.

The work-study mutual aid movement originated with contemporary feminism's pursuit of freedom and liberation. It was inspired by the work-study groups of Chinese students studying in the United States in 1914, and the work-study groups in France in 1915. It was also influenced by Tolstoy's doctrine of pan-labor, Kropotkin's anarchism (especially his theory of mutual aid), and Mushakoji's New Village doctrine. It was a short period of utopian socialism practiced by Chinese left-wing intellectuals before they turned to "scientific socialism." Mushakoji's thought, introduced to China during the May 4th Movement, including egalitarianism and humanitarianism, continued to influence intellectuals in the CPC, including Peng Pai, who was engaged in the Peasant Movement in Haifeng, Guangdong Province, from 1922 to 1927, and Wang Shiwei, who called "for humane and democratic socialism" in the Yan'an period.[8]

Mushakoji may not have imagined that his New Village would have such a significant impact on China. When he received subscription money from Zhou Zuoren for *New Village* magazine in October 1918, he was very excited and full of expectations for the internationalization of the cause. In a poem, he wrote: "Chinese people! Build a New Village branch in China!" When Zhou Zuoren visited New Village in July 1919, Mushakoji had just experienced the internal crisis caused by Kimura Syouta, so he might have regarded the arrival of this Chinese writer as affirmation. In the August issue of the same year, *New Village* published Zhou Zuoren's poetry and the article "Mr. Zhou," about Zhou Zuoren's visit to New Village, by Mushakoji's wife Fusako.[9] In February 1920, Zhou Zuoren established the Beijing branch, which finally allowed Mushakoji to see the

---

[8]. Meng Qingyan, "Diggers and Agitators: On the Peasant Movement in the Early Rural Revolution of the Communist Party," *Society*, vol. 3 no. 37, 2017, pp. 180-214. Gao Hua, *How the Red Sun Rose* (Hong Kong: Chinese University Press, 2000) p. 328.

[9]. Dong Bingyue, "Zhou Zuoren and *New Village* Magazine," *Chinese Modern Literature Research Series*, No. 2, 1998, pp. 162-168. Dong Bingyue's translation of "Mr. Zhou" by Mushakoji Fusako is on pages 156-159.

fruits of his efforts. That same year, Ye Shaojun (Ye Shengtao), who taught at Wu County No. 5 Higher Primary School in Luzhi, Suzhou, became a member of New Village. Li Dazhao recommended a group of Peking University students, including Huang Rikui, Kang Baiqing, Fang Hao, Xu Yanzhi, Meng Shouchun, and others to visit the Tokyo branch of New Village. Later, Li Zongwu and Tong Yixin, members of another Peking University visiting group, and the Labor-Student Association of Peking Normal College, also visited the Tokyo branch, as well as Aranosha. Li Zongwu later translated Mushakoji's book *Human Life*, which was published by Zhonghua Book Company in 1922.[10] These were all Chinese people who had direct relationships with New Village. As the initiator of the spread of New Village in China, Zhou Zuoren made great contributions.

In *The Memoir of Zhitang*, completed in 1962,

---

[10] Ye Shaojun was a member of New Village, and the record of Li Zongwu and Tong Yixin's visit to the Tokyo branch is from Dong Bingyue, "Zhou Zuoren and New Village Magazine"; The record of Huang Renkui, Kang Baiqing, Fang Hao, Xu Yanzhi, and Meng Shouchun's visit to the Tokyo branch is from Wang Xiaoqiu, "Sino-Japanese Cultural Thought and Youth Exchanges During the May Fourth Movement," in Hao Bin and Ouyang Zhesheng eds., *The May Fourth Movement and China in the 20th Century* (Beijing: Social Sciences Literature Press, 2001).

Zhou Zuoren recalls his life—devoting only ten pages to New Village. He mentions a new-style poem, "River" (published in both *New Youth* and *New Village*), written before visiting New Village in 1919, and an old-style poem from 1942, to explain why he believed in the New Village doctrine at that time. Both poems expressed fear of, and concern for, water. The former is 57 lines long, depicting the worries of downstream rice seedlings and mulberry trees due to farmers building dams. The latter is regulated verse: "The life of an old man is to grow vegetables and flowers; he stands at dusk with a tobacco pipe his mouth. Before the pea shoot flowers falls, the melon ripens; he stares at the full clouds south of the mountain." He explained, "I am a person from the southeast of China. We have emotional ties to water, but also know well water's power." For people from Jiangsu and Zhejiang, "full clouds" are omens of a coming flood. Zhou admitted that because his "concern for life, and compassion during chaos," he agreed with Mushakoji's advocacy of a peaceful humanitarian and utopian experiment in order to avoid violent revolution, and he even developed a religious fervor for it.[11] Zhou Zuoren's dream of New Village germinated in the same year as the May 4th Movement, and he didn't awaken from it until five years later.[12] In that passionate era, everyone took on a role—as in the line from the *Book of Songs* about standing helplessly under the "distant and azure Heaven:" "Those who knew me said I was sad at heart; those who did not know me said I was seeking for something"[13]—as if this were the only way to prove that they were the legitimate descendants of the *Book of Songs* and the inheritors of China. Feeling the pain of the times and shouting to the sky for advice was regarded by Zhou Zuoren in his later years as a "common disease of the intellectual class."[14] But the revolution that was doomed to come eventually arrived, like a woman giving birth or like a melon dropping from the vine.

---

11. All above quoted from Zhou Zuoren, *The Memoir of Zhitang* (Hong Kong: Oxford University Press, 2019), pp. 357-367.

12. Ibid. He said: "It wasn't until the spring of 1924, after the publication of *The Uselessness of Lesson*, that I woke up from this delusion."

13. The *Book of Songs*, or *Book of Poetry*, is the oldest existing collection of Chinese poetry dating from the 11th to 7th centuries BC. Here the translation is quoted from "The Shoo Le," *The Odes of Royal Domainn*, Book VI, Part I, The Body of The Volume, *The She King, or The Book of Poetry*, translated by James Legge (Hong Kong: Lane Crawford & Co., London: Trübner & Co.,1871),110-111.

14. Zhou Zuoren, *The Memoir of Zhitang*, pp. 357-367.

The Mushakoji Saneatsu Memorial Museum, Chofu.
Photo by Ou Ning, 2019.

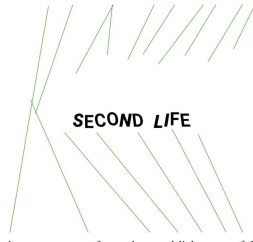

SECOND LIFE

In the seven years from the establishment of New Village in November 1918 to his departure in December 1925, Mushakoji experienced criticism from the "labor faction" in the village and the suspension of the publication of *Shirikaba*, but never abandoned his literary and artistic work. Instead, his rural life in New Village stimulated his creativity. The New Village Publishing Department and Aranosha, established in 1920, became outlets for his literary and artistic activities and creative energy. In addition to the official magazine, *New Village*, which was founded in 1918, they also published the literature and arts magazines *Growing Constellations* (founded

1921), the newsletter *New Village Communications* (founded 1924), the *New Village Series* (a total of 16 volumes published between 1925 and 1928), as well as like-minded magazines specializing in literary and artistic works of New Village members such as *Creation*, *Waste Land*, *Bluebird*, and *Dawn Bird*. In addition to theorizing and writing essays about New Village, Mushakoji also wrote novels—such as *A Happy Man* and *Friendship* in 1919, and biographies like *Jesus*. In 1920, he wrote the documentary work *The Land*, the novel *The Fate of the Third Hermit*, the autobiography *A Certain Man*, and the plays *Buddha and Sun Wukong* and *A Day's Susanoo*. In 1923, he wrote the plays *In Peach Blossom Land* and *Bodhidharma*. In 1924, he wrote the play *The Man Who Values Fate and Go*, and in 1926 he wrote the play *Desire*, among others (he wrote over 6000 novels, plays, poems, and essays throughout his life). Among them, *A Happy Man*, *Jesus*, and *The Fate of the Third Hermit* are known together as the New Village Trilogy. In 1925, New Village established its own press, and half of the profits from publishing and distribution were distributed to the editorial department and printing factory, while the other half was distributed to New

Village headquarters. Mushakoji did not receive any remuneration, and refused any payments. After he left the village and became an outside member, cultural production in New Village remained active. In 1930 they established a theater department and organized the New Village Theater Troupe to perform in Tokyo and other places.

But Mushakoji's literary career began to enter a decade-long slump after moving out of New Village. During this period, the Japanese literary world was dominated by "proletarian literature." In 1926, the Japanese Communist Party, which had been disbanded two years before, was reestablished. Emperor Taisho also died at the end of that year, to be replaced by Crown Prince Hirohito, who took office and renamed the era to Showa. In 1928, the parliamentary implementation of universal suffrage expanded democracy to the grassroots level, and the establishment of the All-Japan Proletarian Art Alliance (NAPF)[1] integrated all left-wing literary and artistic forces. The onset of the Great Depression in 1929 confirmed Marxist predictions about the cyclical

---

1. NAPF is the Italian abbreviation for Nippona Artista Proleta Federacio, for the All-Japan Proletarian Art Alliance.

economic crises of capitalism. Mushakoji's former admirer, Kobayashi Takiji, published the novel *The Crab Cannery Ship*, which became the standard for proletarian literature. In 1930, the workers at the Fuji Knitting Mills in Kanagawa Prefecture went on strike, and Tanabe Kiyoshi faced off against the Tokko police (Special Higher Police) for more than 100 hours from the top of a chimney—eventually forcing the factory to accept bargaining conditions for workers to raise their wages. From then on, "Chimney Man" became synonymous with the labor movement. The remarkable effect of class struggle and society's enthusiastic attention paid to Marxism left Mushakoji, now an outdated writer of the White Birch Society, unemployed. Years later, he still retained bitter memories of the time: "My time of unemployment had arrived. By that time, I was almost 50 years old. *Central Review* and *Reformation* no longer asked for submissions from me. Prior to that, I almost never needed to submit anything. But during that period, if I remained silent, no one would ask me. In that situation, in order to sell a manuscript, I began to seek out help from magazines...I most hoped to get support from Kodansha. Only they did not lean to the left, and were willing to take my work on."[2]

He could only be published by writing historical literary biographies, and passed the time by teaching himself painting (starting from 1927). As he passed the halfway mark of this bleak decade, history began to quietly express a power that would alter his fate. On September 18, 1931, Ishiwara Kanji incited the Mukden Incident. The Kwantung Army occupied the entirety of Northeast China within 100 days, and then established Manchukuo. On May 15, 1932, Inukai Tsuyoshi, the "God of Constitutionalism" and Prime Minister, was killed for opposing war and reducing military spending—historically known as the May 15 Incident. On February 20, 1933, Kobayashi Takiji died of torture after being detained by the Tokko police. Proletarian literature began to ebb. In 1934, Mushakoji published his *Biography of the Buddha* with Kodansha. The book describes the life of the Buddha from the perspective of being a human rather than a deity. It became a best-seller due to its simple and understandable writing, and

---

[2] Mushakoji Saneatsu, *The Path I Have Taken* (Tokyo: Yomiuri Shimbun, 1956), in Liu Lishan, p. 214.

its "purity" (his own claim). Within half a year, it had been reprinted 75 times.[3] On February 26, 1936, the Kodoha (Imperial Way Faction) of the Japanese army mutinied but failed to wipe out the Toseiha (Control Faction). The influence of fascism soared. Japan was steeped in militaristic politics and careened towards World War II. In April of that year, Mushakoji traveled to Europe for the first time at the invitation of his brother, Kintomo, who was serving as the Ambassador of Japan to Germany. Ending his era of disappointments, he was about to embark on his second life. In June 1937, he was elected as a member of the Imperial Art Academy, and a month later, the Marco Polo Bridge Incident happened.[4]

After New Village moved from Kijo to Moroyama in 1938, Mushakoji only returned twice a year, but held frequent solo art exhibitions. In 1942, in accordance with the doctrine of "The New Order

---

[3]. Mushakoji Saneatsu, *Biography of the Buddha*, trans. Dong Xuechang (Beijing: Writer's Publishing House, 2001), Translator's Postscript, p. 264.

[4]. The Marco Polo Bridge Incident, also known as the Lugou Bridge Incident or the July 7 Incident, was a battle during July 1937 in the district of Beijing between China's National Revolutionary Army and the Imperial Japanese Army. It is generally regarded as the start of the Second Sino-Japanese War.

of Greater East Asia," he advocated for Japan's foreign war in *Personal Thoughts on the Great East Asia War*. That year, under the manipulation of the Japanese government's intelligence agency during the war, The Patriotic Association for Japanese Literature was established and held three Greater East Asia Literary Conferences, with participants from Japan's mainland, colonies, and occupied areas. The first was in Tokyo and Osaka in 1942, the second in Tokyo in 1943, and the third in Nanjing in 1944. Mushakoji attended the first two meetings and delivered speeches, but did not attend the third. However, at the third meeting, his speech was read by his colleague from the era of *White Birch*, Nagoya Yoshiro. By that time, Mushakoji had become very different from the Mushakoji who opposed war and violence, and who advocated pacifism and humanitarianism. The reasons for this may be related to what he saw during his European tour. Although he came into contact with the diplomatic community in Germany, Hitler's influence on him was only as a political leader who caused much public excitement. What made him uneasy was that, on a train in Italy, an elderly man was unwilling to sit next to him because he had an Asian face—possibly reinforcing his sense of national humiliation.[5] In 1945, Japan was defeated, and surrendered. In March 1946, Mushakoji was appointed as a member of the House of Peers. But four months later, because of his actions during the war, according to the United Nations Memorandum for the Supreme Commander his crimes were classified as Grade G, that is, "extreme statism or militarism." His office as a member of the House of Peers was terminated along with his previous membership at the Imperial Art Academy. It was not until August 1951 that this "dismissal order" was lifted.

In 1934, during Mushakoji's "time of disappointment," Zhou Zuoren and his wife Hata Nobuko returned to Japan to visit family. He met Mushakoji for the second time in Tokyo. The following experiences of the two eventually led towards similar fates. Zhou Zuoren did not move south with Peking University in 1937, but stayed in Beijing while it was under Japanese occupation. In 1938, he became a visiting professor at Yenching

---

[5]. Tessa Morris-Suzuki, "Beyond Utopia: New Villages and Living Politics in Modern Japan and across Frontiers."

University, with its religious sponsorship, and attended the Symposium on Revitalizing Chinese Cultural Construction sponsored by the *Japan Daily News*. In 1939, he was shot and wounded by a would-be assassin—and was afterwards protected by the military police at his home.[6] Later, he accepted an appointment letter from Wang Jingwei and the Nanjing government to be director of the National Peking University Library. In 1940, he was appointed by the Wang Jingwei regime as a Standing Member of the North China Administrative Committee and Supervisor of the General Education Administration. In 1941, he also served as the President of the East Asia Cultural Agreement Association and went to Tokyo for a meeting where he met with Mushakoji

---

6. The assassin arrived at Zhou Zuoren's home claiming that he was part of a Sino-Japanese Institute. It was set up by "China expert" Doihara Kenji in 1925 in Tianjin and included professors at Peking University, Zhou Zuoren and Li Dazhao. By 1939, Doihara Kenji had become the Commander of the Fifth Army of the Kwantung Army. By referring to this incident, did that mean the assassin was anti-Japanese? As for the identity of the assassin, Zhou Zuoren said in *The Memoir of Zhitang* that "although the Japanese military and police tried their best to frame this as being a Kuomintang spy, in fact they did it themselves...I went to Yenching to be a guest professor, refusing invitations from all other schools. It was very obvious who was offended by this." See pp. 538-539.

for the third time. In 1942, he visited Manchukuo with Wang Jingwei, and participated in the Ten-Year Anniversary. In 1943, Mushakoji went to Nanjing to participate in a series of activities for the Sino-Japanese Cultural Association, and the two met for a fourth time in Beijing. Zhou Zuoren later served as the Vice-Chairman of the North China Comprehensive Investigation and Research Institute. In 1944, he served concurrently as Director of the Sino-Japanese Cultural Association. In December 1945, he was arrested by the Chiang Kai-Shek government on charges of treason and escorted to Nanjing for trial. He was imprisoned at the Tiger Bridge Prison until his release in 1949.[7] Zhou

---

[7] As for this "stain on his life," Zhou Zuoren had no explanation in *The Memoir of Zhitang*. Neither did he provide an explanation for his conflict with Lu Xun. But he did mention that the four "Japan's Perspectives" written between 1935 and 1937 had analysis and criticism of Japan's "mainland policy" (pp. 524-531), and that his "China's Ideological Issues," written in 1942, was attacked by Kataoka Teppei, the writer of the Patriotic Association for Japanese Literature, who accused Zhou of encouraging Chinese people not to cooperate with the "New Order of Greater East Asia," and accused him of being a "reactionary writer" (pp. 543-555). Yet, by using the logic of "my enemy's enemy," Zhou Zuoren was actually defending himself. This kind of defense first appeared in a letter he wrote to the head of the Central Committee of the Communist Party of China in 1949, which can be found in the appendix of the Oxford edition of *The Memoir of Zhitang*, pp. 677-689.

Zuoren lived in Beijing in his later years, passing away on May 6, 1967 due to illness.

In his later years, Mushakoji and his wife Meshigawa Yasuko settled in Iruma, Chofu (today Wakaba). After witnessing the death of his old friends Yanagi Soetsu, Nagayo Yoshiro, Shiga Naoya, and his brother and his wife, he died on April 9, 1976. His former residence has been fully preserved. It is a traditional Japanese residential building that covers an area of nearly 200 square meters, built on a slope. The walls are coated with plaster, with an iron gabled roof construction. The interior is an emerging style in the postwar period, the Sukiya style—hidden between trees and ponds—and it is indeed a secluded place. In 1955, Mushakoji and his wife selected this site, known as Sengawa, and asked architect Yamaguti Hosyun to design and build their wooden home. They lived there for more than 20 years afterwards. In 1978, Chofu set aside 5000 square meters of land next to the former residence to create a traditional Japanese garden called Saneatsu Park. In 1985, it invited Le Corbusier's student Sakakura Junzo and his architectural firm to build the Saneatsu Mushakoji Memorial Museum in the style of contemporary

Japanese Minka,[8] collecting and displaying a large number of manuscripts, documents, photos, videos, publications and paintings of Mushakoji's, as well as artworks collected by him, and donated by his descendents. When I visited, the museum was being renovated. Fortunately, the archives and library were still open, allowing me to browse through a large number of publications and digital materials.

---

[8] Minka, "house of the people," is a vernacular house constructed in traditional Japanese building styles.

The village elder Watanabe Kanzi's 1981 calligraphy "On Happiness" (central) and Mushakoji Saneatsu's 1953 calligraphy on the pillar, "No other road allows me to survive; I will walk this road"(right), in the visitor reception room, Moroyama.
Photo by Ou Ning, 2019.

POSTWAR YEARS

When New Village first moved from Kijo to Moroyama in 1938, it was still a wilderness area. They held a reclamation ceremony on September 17, 1939, which was also designated as the opening day of New Village at Moroyama. On that day, Mushakoji arrived from his nearby residence at Mitaka, Kitatama, to attend the ceremony. He holds a small axe in the commemorative photo, with the ten members who participated in the reclamation. In 1941, New Village at Moroyama founded a new official magazine called *Potato*, replacing the original *New Village*. However, in 1944, due to wartime policies, it was forcibly incorporated into *Literature Japan*. Affected by World

War II, the number of members in New Village continued to decrease, and by the end of the war only one household with five members remained. After the war, the number of people who joined the group gradually increased again. In 1947, *Sunflower* was founded, and New Village resumed the tradition of holding anniversary celebrations every five years. On the occasion of the 30th anniversary in 1948, New Village at Moroyama obtained the qualification of public interest incorporated foundation and became a legitimate social organization recognized, protected, and supported by the government. The magazine *New Village* resumed publication, and they founded a new magazine, *Heart*. Operating as a foundation reduced the dependence on Mushakoji's personal donations, and finally relieved the financial burden on New Village. In 1953, New Village celebrated its 35th anniversary and built new collective dormitories, Shirakawa Village (for men) and Kadokawa Village (for women). Mushakoji returned to Moroyama and wrote a poem on a pillar with a brush, "No other road allows me to survive; I will walk this road." Today, the pillar is kept in the village's visitor reception room. In 1963, New Village at Kijo also became a corporate legal entity, but was dissolved in 2014 due to being deemed not in the public interest during the 2006 reform of public interest corporations.

Thanks to the gradual recovery of Japan's economy after the war, New Village at Moroyama began to develop a chicken farming industry and by the 1960's achieved great success. Its golden period came in the 1970s and 1980s. In 1976, when Mushakoji passed away, it produced 25,000 eggs per day and had 60 members in the village, resulting in a financial surplus.[1] Those who joined New Village during the 1960s to 1970s were all from the working class. At that time, young intellectuals were busy with radical left-wing student activism, and regarded New Village as a historical relic of bourgeois humanitarianism, or a naive petit bourgeois dream. A survey in 1989 showed that most of the village members used to work as land surveyors, factory technicians, accountants, bakers, drivers, and farm laborers.[2] They all joined New Village to avoid the pressures of the capitalist world during the Iwato

---

[1] Tessa Morris-Suzuki, "Beyond Utopia."
[2] Ibid.

Boom, the Olympic Boom, the Izanagi Boom, and other periods of rapid economic growth in Japan. In the 1980s, Japan became the second largest economy in the world. Hot money accumulated in the domestic consumption market, and money from real estate transactions poured into the world market. People madly bought overseas stocks, bonds, real estate, works of art, and luxury goods, creating a large economic bubble. After 1990, when the bubble burst, the economy deteriorated, and Japan entered its "lost decade." During this period, due to the decline in egg prices and a lack of manpower, the income from raising chickens in New Village at Moroyama again reached a low, and they needed to find new ways to survive.

At different times, New Village tried new agricultural and handicraft projects. In addition to raising chickens and cows, it also cultivated rice, vegetables, tea, fruit, mushrooms, and produced charcoal and pottery. Even in the toughest times, New Village still adhered to the spirit of combining work and rest, with only six hours of labor per day (two hours less than when Mushakoji started the village at Koji), one day off per week, and leisure time to develop oneself through art and other activities. The system of collective ownership of property, free food and accommodations, medical care, and personal allowance distribution continued as usual. Artist Watanabe Osamu joined the village in 1955, and created paintings and sculptures in addition to his voluntary labor; he also taught an art class in the village. Potter Watanabe Kanezirou entered the village in 1959 and built a Taizan kiln there. Since 1971, he has accepted commissions from outside the village to produce ceramic works. He has also held exhibitions in Tokyo and other places, substantially increasing income for New Village. By 1981, the annual income of New Village was close to 400 million yen, with nearly 70 members in the village—reaching a historical peak, and then gradually declining again.[3]

According to Dong Bingyue, who studied at the University of Tokyo for his doctorate and is a researcher at the Institute of Literature of the Chinese Academy of Social Sciences, during his visit in 2004 the monthly allowance for each member of New Village was 35,000 yen, but some members

---

3. *100 Years of New Village: 1918-2018*, p. 66.

expressed regrets that New Village failed to provide additional travel allowances. At that time, there were 25 members in the village, including 16 who were near the age of 60 and only five under the age of 50. There were over 300 outside members in Japan.[4] Dong Bingyue is a scholar of Mushakoji and Zhou Zuoren. During his studies in Tokyo in 1996, he made his first visit to New Village at Moroyama, and applied to join as an outsider member. It is said that there were three Chinese members including him at that time, all of whom were graduates of Beijing University.[5] In the century-old history of New Village, apart from the members of an early Dalian branch who were not necessarily Chinese, these three were the first new Chinese members since Zhou Zuoren and Ye Shaojun. According to Lin Hengqing's research, Yuan Suyi from Shufang Township, Jianyang City, Fujian Province, wanted to build a New Village on his own land in his hometown of Taiyangshan. He went to New Village at Koji for a trial period in 1930, and became

---

[4]. Dong Bingyue, "The Last Oasis: Japan's New Village Today," *21st Century*, no. 88, April 2005, pp. 113-121.

[5]. Dong Bingyue, "Zhou Zuoren and New Village Magazine," *Chinese Modern Literature Research Series*.

the only known Chinese member in the village at the time.[6]

When Dong Bingyue visited New Village at Moroyama for the second time, in 2004, village elder Watanabe Kanzi was 94 years old and in his twilight years. He became a member outside the village in 1928 and moved inside in 1946. He experienced the prosperity of New Village after the war and served as its chairman from 1988 to 1994. He lived in the village from beginning to end. Unlike Watanabe Kanzi, his successor, Isimura Seimei, left the village and moved back to Tokyo in 1954 (this trend was actually begun by Mushakoji), leading the work of New Village through the Tokyo branch until 2016. The Tokyo branch has a New Village Hall in Jimbo Village, with meetings on the first Sunday of each month and a weekly meeting every Thursday to discuss New Village affairs. In fact, it has become the manager of the Moroyama headquarters. Times have changed, and New Village has also changed. Some people still use New Village as a refuge from

---

[6] Lin Hengqing, "The New Village Movement of Mushakoji Saneatsu and its Influence on Zhou Zuoren," Fujian Normal University master's thesis, 2001; in Zhao Hong, *The Chinese Dream of a New Village*, p. 10.

setbacks in the outside world. But this is quite different from the original intention of Mushakoji, to create an island which could in turn influence the outside world.

New Village had a huge impact on people when it first emerged. Those who joined New Village as members in the early stages, even though they had mobility and could come and go, experienced New Village playing a decisive role in the direction of their lives. Although Kimura Syouta left because of disagreements with Mushakoji, he moved to Toyama in Chiba Prefecture in 1925 to continue his semi-agricultural life of "sunny farming and rainy reading."[7] The "White Birch School Teacher" Kobayashi Tatsue left due to a serious illness, but he continued to promote Mushakoji's idealism until his death at the age of 104. Although the novelist Nirayama Keisuke found life at Kijo very difficult, he believed that he benefited greatly from physical labor. Novelist Shigeho Mera appears in the only group photo of the founding members of New Village at Kijo (taken in 1919). In 1929, he announced the launch of an international plan for Love Village,

---

[7.] *100 Years of New Village: 1918-2018*, p. 14.

influenced by New Village. Although it never materialized, some of those who responded to it set off to Brazil to search for a site to build the first Love Village; one person even went to the jungles of Myanmar to negotiate 3000 hectares of rent-free land as the location of the second Love Village. After leaving New Village, poet Ito Isao returned to his hometown in Iwate Prefecture to cultivate land for farming. In 1968, he and his family moved to a remote area in eastern Paraguay, where he founded a small self-reliant commune.[8]

When I went to New Village at Moroyama, I didn't understand the current situation of its internal operations. In terms of quickly-formed impressions, it seemed to face the same problems of the graying population in ordinary rural areas of Japan. Since 2000, under the influence of the Japanese government's policy of "focusing on agriculture with new rules,"[9] young people in urban areas have become interested in the so-called "half-agriculture, half-X" lifestyle—that is, moving to

---

8. Tessa Morris-Suzuki, "Beyond Utopia."
9. The policy of providing assistance through government agencies or other entities and welcoming people from various backgrounds to join the agricultural workers.

rural areas but not as full-time farmers, in order to engage in self-sufficient small-scale farming while also engaging in freelance work that they enjoy. The "X" refers to "unknown talent." It is the exploration of one's own potential after being freed from the shackles of going into a salaried workplace. It can be substituted with various freelance jobs. For example, if you plant vegetables while also writing articles for magazines, you are "half-farmer and half-writer." Advocates of half-agriculture, half-X believe that it is not only a new lifestyle for the 21st century, but also supplies a new worldview and values.[10] But these young people do not patronize the historical utopia of New Village at Moroyama. There is indeed no vast countryside there that can be put on Instagram, nor are there ancient houses in the mountains that can be transformed into enviable homestays or cafes. All that is there is the old collective system and the struggle with the land. But the more fundamental reason lies in ideological barriers. As the pioneer of semi-rural life more than a century ago, New

---

10. Shiomi Naoki, *The Life of Half-Agriculture and Half-X: Follow Nature and Practice Talent*, trans. Su Fengya (Taipei: Commonwealth Publishing, 2006), p. 35.

Village was more radical than today's theory of half-agriculture and half-X—not to mention the left-wing student activism of the 1960s and 1970s, which was doubly radical. In 1974, Oda Makoto, a well-known writer, supported the plan of Oyama Hachisaburo, who called himself a "revolutionary,"[11.] to establish a handicrafts commune in Hidaka, near Moroyama. This site implied approaching and inheriting the legacy of New Village. However, it foundered—while New Village still lives.

---

11. The ad copy for the book *Revolutionary Oyama Hachisaburo* is: "The autobiography of Oyama Hachisaburo, the modern Ryoma Sakamoto, who created the blueprint for an ideal society."

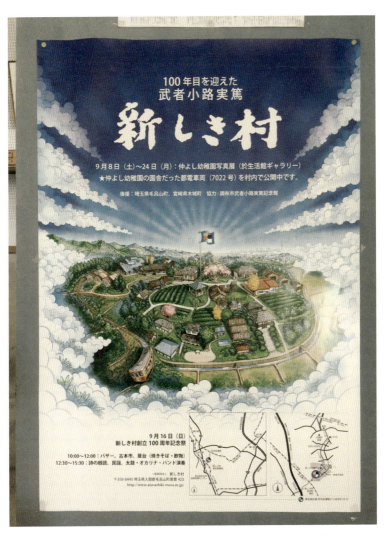

The centennial celebration poster of New Village (1918-2018),
New Village Life and Culture Museum, Moroyama.

Photo by Ou Ning, 2019.

Mushakoji Saneatsu (right) and Shiga Naoya (left) on the trip from Mount Fuji in Yamanashi Prefecture to Mount Akagi in Gunma Prefecture, 1906.

© The Mushakoji Saneatsu Memorial Museum, Chofu

Around 50 members of the White Birch Society, and members of the New Village, attended the grand farewell party at Mushakoji Saneatsu's home in Abiko. September 15, 1918.
© The Mushakoji Saneatsu Memorial Museum, Chofu

The founding members of New Village at Kijo, 1919. From the left in the back row, the fourth is novelist Shigeho Mera, the sixth is Mushakoji Saneatsu.
© The Mushakoji Saneatsu Memorial Museum, Chofu

Mushakoji Saneatsu harvesting wheat, 1919.
© The Mushakoji Saneatsu Memorial Museum, Chofu

The 10th anniversary of the magazine Shirakaba, Tokyo, 1920. From the left in the front row, the first is Yanagi Soetsu, the third is Mushakoji Saneatsu. From the right in the back row, the third is Shiga Naoya, and the eighth is Bernard Leach.
© The Mushakoji Saneatsu Memorial Museum, Chofu

Mushakoji Saneatsu at the study in Kijo, 1924.
© The Mushakoji Saneatsu Memorial Museum, Chofu

The New Village at Kijo, 1935.

© The Mushakoji Saneatsu Memorial Museum, Chofu

When New Village first moved from Kijo to Moroyama in 1938, it was still a wilderness area. They held a reclamation ceremony on September 17, 1939, which was also designated as the opening day of New Village at Moroyama. Mushakoji Saneatsu holds a small axe in the commemorative photo.

© The Mushakoji Saneatsu Memorial Museum, Chofu

In 1953, New Village celebrated its 35th anniversary. Mushakoji Saneatsu returned to Moroyama and wrote a poem on a pillar with a brush, "No other road allows me to survive; I will walk this road."
© The Mushakoji Saneatsu Memorial Museum, Chofu

The New Village at Moroyama, 1976.
© The Mushakoji Saneatsu Memorial Museum, Chofu

The tea garden of Moroyama.
Photo by Ou Ning, 2019.

AGRICULTURAL FUNDAMENTALISM

Looking back from today, the trend of half-agriculture, half-X pursued by young people in Japan is in reality just a repetition of the ideas and practices their predecessors deduced from the Meiji, Taisho, and Showa periods. However, they are disengaged from politics, while their predecessors were closely intertwined with a politics that even evolved into war. In fact, the Greater East Asia War initiated by Japan in the early days of the Showa was related to the heavily agriculturalist thought that was a reaction against capitalism in the early Meiji era, the semi-agricultural experiments of intellectuals that began in the late Meiji era, the New Village Movement that began in the early days of Taisho era, and the Agricultural Fundamentalism (*Nohonshugi*) of the early days of the Showa—together like waves.

The political theory of "New Order in Greater East Asia" that endorsed the Greater East Asia War held much fascination for some Asian intellectuals at that time. It originated from the "Argument for Leaving Asia (*Datsu-A Ron*)," written by Fukuzawa Yukichi in 1885, which stated that, under an invincible Western civilization, Japan had reformed and become strong, leaving Asia behind and entering Europe. However, neighboring China and Korea were reluctant to make progress and were mired in Confucianism—which would only drag Japan backwards. According to the essay, Japan should adopt the attitudes of European and American powers, and use war to shake awake, and to innovate.[1] An implied theory of Asian federation (*Tongyang Yondaeron*) was later interpreted to be a Pan-Asianism of mutually dependent nations. Japan is a small country with limited land and mineral

---

1. Fukuzawa's original essay "Datsu-A Ron" is reprinted in *Fukuzawa Yukichi Zenshu*, Vol. 10 (Tokyo: Iwanami Shoten, 1960), pp.238-240. An English version is available in David Lu, ed., *Japan: A Documentary History* (Armonk: M.E. Sharpe, 1997), pp. 351-353.

resources, but it gained confidence after the Meiji Restoration, the Sino-Japanese War, and the Russo-Japan War. Because of the destruction of the 1923 Great Kanto Earthquake and the Showa Depression caused by the Great Depression in 1929, Japan began to seek further external expansion—for example with the Mukden Incident of 1931 and the Marco Polo Bridge Incident of 1937. For the needs of war mobilization, Pan-Asianism was repackaged by militarists and fascists as the noble cause of "liberating" Asian nations from the colonial rule of European and American powers—to achieve common prosperity. In 1938, Japanese Prime Minister Konoe Fumimaro called for the establishment of a "New Order in Greater East Asia." In 1940, he proposed the establishment of the Greater East Asia Co-Prosperity Sphere, including the political territories of Japan, Korea, Taiwan, Sakhalin, the Kwantung Leased Territory, the South Seas Mandate, Manchukuo, the Mengjiang United Autonomous Government, the Wang Jingwei regime, French Indochina, Thailand, Burma, British Malaya and Borneo, the Dutch East Indies, Portuguese Timor, and the Second Philippine Republic. This promise of coexistence and mutual prosperity may also have been one of the reasons for the transformation of Mushakoji's thought and Zhou Zuoren's defection.

Pan-Asianism developed from the Revive Asia Society (*Koa-kai*)'s Asian Revivalism and Tarui Tokichi's theory of Great Eastern Federation to Kodera Kenkichi's ideology of Greater Asia and Tokutomi Soho's Asian Monroe Doctrine. It was finally synthesized by Okawa Shumei as the theory of the Greater East Asia Co-Prosperity Sphere, which emphasized Japan's leadership in Asia, and emphasized Japan's well-being for Asia's overall interests. Thus, in the Greater East Asia War, militarists had shrines built in occupied areas, promoted Shinto and the authority of the Mikado, and required schools to teach Japanese as the common language of East Asia. In the process of the development of Pan-Asianism and the theory of the Greater East Asia Co-Prosperity Sphere, Agricultural Fundamentalism, an important vein of Japanese modern thought, provided indispensable nutrients.

Agriculturalism has a long history in Asia. It originated in China in the mythical Shennong period and has continued to spread, being shared by Confucian circles throughout East Asia. But the Japanese Agricultural Fundamentalism mentioned here mainly refers to the anti-capitalist physiocracy that emerged in the Meiji Restoration. In the early and middle Meiji period, the representative figures were Maeda Masana (former Minister of Agriculture and Commerce), Shinagawa Yajiro (former Minister of Home Affairs), Hirata Tosuke (former Minister of Agriculture and Commerce), and Tani Tateki (soldier and politician). In the late Meiji and the Taisho, there were Yokoi Tokiyoshi (agricultural economist), Yanagita Kunio (father of Japanese folklore studies), Yamazaki Nobuyoshi (agronomist), Kawakami Hajime (translator of *Das Kapital* and Marxist economist), Ishiguro Tadaatsu (former Minister of Agriculture and Forestry, known as the "god of agriculture"), and Okada Narau (former Director of the of Imperial Library). During the Showa period, before the outbreak of World War II, the names include Gondo Seikyo (a scholar of East Asian policy), Nagano Akira (former Chairman of the Central Committee of the Farmers Association, and expert on China), Tachibana Kozaburo (right-wing activist), Kato Kazuo (poet, critic, Tolstoyist), Kato Kanji (educator, kendo practitioner), and Nasu Shiroshi (agricultural economics scholar). In addition, there were many other Japanese intellectuals with similar ideas.

Unlike Ogyu Sorai, a Japanese Confucian scholar who paid attention to agriculture before the Meiji Restoration, or agricultural policy scholars Ninomiya Sontoku and Ohara Yugaku, these new agriculturalists had strong "anti-modern, anti-Western, anti-urban, anti-big industry, and anti-centralization" tendencies.[2] The conditions were similar to the early days of the first Industrial Revolution in Britain: Under the new policies of "promotion of industry"(*shokusan-kogyo*) and "land tax reform (*chisokaisei*)," land became centralized through free trade, and landless farmers became tenant farmers or workers in new factories due to an inability to pay rent. Landowners invested land profits into financial markets or started industries and became capitalists. Agriculture was squeezed by industry and commerce, urbanization continued to

---

[2] Liu Feng, "The Relevance of Modern Japanese Agricultural Fundamentalism and Asianism," *World History*, no. 2, 2015, pp. 78-87.

expand, rural areas gradually went bankrupt, wealth inequality intensified, and farmers faced a tragic situation—but their resistance increased. In the eyes of the agriculturalist intellectuals who cared about the sufferings of common folk, the Meiji Restoration left the "national essence" of Japan behind.

Because "building the nation through agriculture" was the tradition in Japan as well as throughout East Asia, what was destroying that tradition was modern Western capitalism, industrialization, and urbanization. Therefore, adhering to agriculturalism became symbolic of resistance to these destructive forces, and was the starting point for reconstructing the "Japanese spirit" and the "East Asian spirit." This also left the door open to fascism, Pan-Asianism, and the Greater East Asia Co-Prosperity Sphere to absorb agriculturalism. Because it was anti-Western, agriculturalism not only defied capitalism, but also Marxism. It only believed in a political system that was compatible with Asia's traditional agrarian society, that is, where imperial power and rural autonomy were both paramount. This also provided a historical basis for the emperor as a symbol of imperial leadership in the Greater

East Asia Co-Prosperity Sphere, under which all countries would live in harmony but also take charge of their own politics, as "unifying all the world under one roof"(*hakko ichiu*). However, the reason why Agricultural Fundamentalism truly became Japan's national policy at the time was the impact of the Showa Depression on rural areas.

In 1929, the Great Depression happened in the United States, leading to a sharp decrease in Japanese exports of raw silk and other agricultural products to the United States, and a drop in prices. By 1930, the contraction of the overseas market, together with a domestic deflation policy and a fall in rice prices caused by a bumper rice harvest, triggered the first bumper year famine in rural areas in the history of Japan. Raw silk and rice were the most important pillars of Japanese agriculture, and after these two sources of income were cut off, rural areas suffered a devastating blow. In 1931, the two important agricultural and fishing areas of the Tohoku Region and Hokkaido suffered rare severe cold damage, which made things worse. The impact of the financial crisis on cities also greatly reduced employment opportunities, forcing many people to return to agriculture, greatly squeezing farmers' livelihoods. In many places there was no food to eat, and they could only rely on dried goods (like sardines or other small fish that were dried and used as fertilizer), husks, and wild vegetables to satisfy their hunger. There were more than 200,000 children who were short of food across the country. In the Tohoku Region and Nagano Prefecture, there was the very serious phenomena of parents selling their children and women selling their bodies for survival. This was the agricultural side of the Showa Depression.

Faced with such a crisis, Agricultural Fundamentalists began to redouble their voices and protest. From 1931 to 1932, Gondo Seikyo, Nagano Akira, Tachibana Kozaburo, Kato Kazuo, Mushakoji Saneatsu, Shimonaka Yasaburo (President of Heiminsha and leader of peasants movement), Ono Takeo (agricultural economist), Okamoto Rikichi (social activist), Kon Toko (Tiantai monk and novelist), Inuta Shigeru (novelist), Nakazawa Benjiro (peasant activist), Inamura Ryuichi (peasant activist), Wago Tsuneo (founder of the Mizuho Agricultural School) and others successively established the Japanese Village Governance Alliance, the Nohon

Alliance, and the Autonomous Farmers' Association. Although they sometimes disagreed, they were all committed to implementing agricultural autonomy in order to promote rural self-reliance. As a charismatic leader, Gondo Seikyo also published *On the History of the Japanese Agricultural System*, *On the Joint Governance of the Emperor and the People*, *A Study of Japan's Earthquake and Famine*, *On Rural Self-reliance* and other works that responded to the difficulties of the times. Advocating rural autonomy had always been his focus, and his famous "theory of state autonomy" had a significant impact on the policy orientation of the Japanese government later on. Its focus was "governing through nature:" "Governing by nature does not mean being governed by wise men, nor by strong men, nor has it anything to do with the punishment of ghosts and gods, or the blessings of the Buddha. Instead, it lies in each person's own nature, inspiring their being, and moving towards autonomy within one's own self-control, leading to neighboring co-governance, rural co-governance, and the rule of regions and nations throughout the world, by not relying on others for that governance."[3] This ideology of rural autonomy when amplified to a region is localism; enlarged to a nation it is sovereigntism; enlarged to Asia it is the Asian Monroe Doctrine. It prepared the fuel of idealism for use in the machine of ideology and strategic deployment across the Greater East Asia Co-Prosperity Sphere.

Under immense pressure, the Japanese government had to take relief measures. Internally, it launched the Rural Economic Revitalization Campaign in 1932. That same year, it decided to conduct "agricultural migration" to Manchukuo. This could be seen as a victory for the Agricultural Fundamentalists. The main policy of the Rural Economic Revitalization Campaign was to select 1000 towns and villages annually for economic subsidies, and to establish economic revitalization committees within these towns and villages which were responsible for rectifying the distribution and utilization of land, improving rural finances and agricultural management organizations, reasonably

---

[3]. Gondo Seikyo, "The Gradual Transformation of Customs and the Origin of Legislative Institutions," *Central Review*, June 1932. Quoted in Liu Feng, "The Relevance of Modern Japanese Agricultural Fundamentalism and Asianism."

arranging labor and production costs, preventing various disasters, and promoting the improvement of living standards. In 1940, in order to promote agricultural research, the Rural Culture Association Japan was established, chaired by Minister of Agriculture and Forestry Arima Yoriyasu. This association has continued operating to this day, and has become a public interest corporation dedicated to agricultural publishing in Japan. The Rural Economic Revitalization Campaign continued until 1943, involving over 80% of the country's towns and villages. However, in reality, financial subsidies were very limited, making it more like an emergency measures public relations campaign. Subsequently, it transitioned to the Campaign for Imperial Rural Establishment. The latter was a policy of building nationalism in rural areas to meet the needs of foreign wars. It inherited the organizational achievements of the former, established a unified mechanism for rural areas that covered all territories, and provided guarantees for any war mobilization, including food supply and military manpower resources. It was the precursor of the later National Spiritual Mobilization Movement and the Taisei

Yokusankai Movement, and was also the starting point for a fascist-dominated system.

In terms of transporting agricultural migrants to Manchukuo, the Japanese government planned to use a policy of one-time subsidies along with tax exemption for ten years to mobilize five million Japanese to migrate in stages. This suggestion was first put forward by the Agricultural Fundamentalist Kato Kanji, who graduated from Tokyo Imperial University of Agriculture and converted from Christianity to Shinto. He believed that, in the agricultural panic, migration to Manchukuo would be a way out for many who found life in Japan difficult. For the Japanese government, transporting agricultural migrants to Manchukuo could alleviate the pressures of hunger and produce agricultural products for Japan that in the future would ensure the food supply of the country. In 1932, this proposal was passed by the National Diet, and Kato Kanji was subsequently appointed head of Manchukuo Pioneer Village. The following year, Uchida Yoshikazu, the architect who designed much of the campus of Tokyo Imperial University, handed over a plan for Manchukuo Pioneer Village: In the middle of a vast land, a square settlement of massive scale appears like a utopia. The most central position is a large building of homocentric squares that looks like the "parallelogram palace" Robert Owen wanted built in New Harmony. Surrounded by a circular area, eight thoroughfares radiate outwards and rows of uniform residences form a spectacular array across the plot.[4] Japanese architects had never had the opportunity to design such a large-scale project—although in the end, this plan was not completed. But by 1945, 1.66 million people had migrated from Japan to Manchukuo. This included more than 860 agricultural development missions, with 320,000 people.

---

4. The drawings can be found in the collection of the Mori Art Museum, *Metabolism, the City of the Future: Dreams and Visions of Reconstruction in Postwar and Present-Day Japan.* (Tokyo: Shinkenchiku, 2011), p. 19.

The memorial statue of Miyazawa Kenji near the restored building of Rasuchijin Association in the Hanamaki Agricultural High School.
Photo by Ou Ning, 2019.

SEMI-AGRICULTURAL LIFE

Before agricultural fundamentalism was absorbed into the ideology of the Empire of Japan and transformed into concrete policies, many intellectuals were already practicing a return to rural life. In 1904, with the support of the Heiminsha, Hara Neki, Fukao Sho, Watanabe Shotaro, and about a dozen other people, leased approximately 12 hectares of land in Makkari Village, Abuta, Hokkaido for land reclamation, creating the Heiminsha Farm and implementing a socialist style of joint-farming. The food they originally planned to produce there was to be returned to the Heiminsha headquarters in Tokyo, but in the first year less than two hectares of arable land were cultivated. The surrounding farmers mocked the group of socialists from Tokyo as "fake farmers," and the local police looked down on them. In the second year, they continued to work hard to gradually eliminate the prejudices against them. Even the police began to help, and the yield of crops greatly increased. In addition to farming, they held slideshows on the farm and at nearby villages to raise money to donate to Yanaka Village, which had been poisoned due to proximity to the Ashio Copper Mine. In addition, they also provided free accommodations for farmers and impoverished tenants who had lost their land due to debt. However, that same year a fire broke out, burning down their buildings, and they had to borrow money to rebuild while continuing to cultivate the land. By 1906 the farm could no longer sustain itself and it was disbanded.

In the same year as the dissolution of the Heiminsha Farm, writer Tokutomi Roka (pen name of Tokutomi Kenjiro) went on a pilgrimage to Jerusalem and then traveled to the Asnaya Polyana manor in Russia to visit Tolstoy. Tokutomi was a Christian, and wrote a book called *Tales of Tolstoy* in 1897, influencing many White Birch writers including Mushakoji. In 1907, he went to Chitose in Musashino, Kitatama, to buy land and a house in a place called Kasuya. He and his family followed Tolstoy's example and started living a rural life. Six years later, he wrote in a letter to a friend, "In these six years, on less than one hectare of land, I have planted trees, sowed seeds, built houses, sweated, used my own feces, and buried the dogs, cats, and chickens that died here. Now, this land is like my own clothes, even my own skin to me. I deeply love this land, where living is peaceful and leaving is painful—and I cannot imagine what it would feel like to lose it."[1] He claimed he was a "beautiful farmer" who observed nature with the meticulousness of a naturalist, and expressed his understanding of the heavens and earth like a haiku poet. At the same time, he also strove to overcome the hardships of rural reality. No matter what, this "earthed life" in the suburbs of Tokyo made him happy.

Tokutomi's love for rural areas and agriculture did not translate into nationalism or Pan-Asianism.

---

1. Tokutomi Kenjiro, "To An Old Friend," *The Babble of Earthworms* (Tokyo: Shinbashido Shoten, 1913).

Like Tolstoy, he was a pacifist and humanist—and he had broken off relations with his famous brother Tokutomi Soho for many years. However, during the High Treason Incident he was indignant over the death of Kotoku Shusui, and built a memorial shrine for him. His migration to the countryside was entirely a personal act. At a time when his family was struggling with polluted and dirty water in their well, and the inability to sleep because of summer mosquito attacks, more Japanese intellectuals also began to practice semi-agricultural life under his influence. This gradually developed into a communitarian utopian movement in rural areas. In terms of ideological orientation, they (including Tokutomi) were all Agricultural Fundamentalists, but not everyone was associated with fascism, Pan-Asianism, or the Greater East Asian Co-Prosperity Sphere (Mushakoji went down this path later on). Their ideological spectrum was diverse, and some of them were fierce opponents of the imperial system, nationalism, and militarism.

In 1911, Eto Tekirei, who was born in Aomori and studied law at Imperial University of Tokyo, moved to Funabashi, Chitose, with his wife

Sekimura Miki and eldest son Kura. With the help of Tokutomi he rented a piece of land with a young friend, Kodaira Hideo, and established the Farmers' Training Ground of Love, leading a self-sufficient life. Eto Tekirei was also a Christian who followed Tolstoy, deeply loved Kropotkin, and followed the teachings of Soto Zen. He viewed the farm as a "hall of meditation between heaven and earth"(*tenchi zendo*), and thought that studying Zen actually meant being a farmer bent over the earth—selfless labor was meditation. In 1913, he moved the farm to Kami-Takaido and renamed it the Three Convolvuluses Farm. The three convolvuluses not only referred to Eto, Sekimura, and Kodaira, but also was the Sekimura family crest. There, they sold the fruit, flowers, and eggs they produced to the political group Baibunsha, founded by Sakai Toshihiko, and socialized with the poet Takamura Kotaro, artist Takata Hiroatsu (who also had created a communal village in Shimo-Takaido), novelist Nakazato Kaizan, poet Ozaki Kihachi, and author Mizuno Yoshu. They spent time talking, and sometimes working together, making Takaido Village a welcoming place for intellectuals at the time.

While training himself for farming, Eto also began to devote himself to his own agricultural theory, the Wheel of Home Farming. He developed his concept of the "home-state" from Gondo Seikyo's theory of the "autonomous state," believing that a home rooted in local soil was a "state," and that "home farming" rooted the production and operations of agriculture in a certain place. The concept of the "farming wheel" came from the Buddhist concept of the Wheel of the Dharma, and he regarded farming and rural living as spiritual vehicles, like boats that crossed to the other shore of a life. He liked to invent new terms to explain his ideas through mind mapping. The Wheel of Home Farming includes eight sub-concepts related to agricultural philosophy, religious belief, agricultural divisions of labor, production methods, and autonomous systems and social organizations: the agricultural Dao; agricultural thought; agricultural education; the agricultural soul; agricultural practice; agricultural law; agricultural systems; and agricultural organizations. These are interwoven with Historia Regionalis, Feldologie, Syndikatologie, and Tatologie—to form a platform of wisdom and merit, the Agrayana Orbis Mandrus.[2] On this basis, Eto later further developed Fieldism, meaning that a specific place's "field" could become a shared and symbiotic field that triggered subjectivity, and that a such field could supply one's life journey. This idea was quite similar to that of Liang Shuming, his contemporary from the group of Chinese rural reconstructionists. Japanese scholar Kimura Hiroshi even conducted a comparative study between the Wheel of Home Farming and Liang Shuming's theories.[3]

Eto Tekirei published *A Farmer's Home* in 1922, where he shared his experiences. He received widespread attention for it, and many people went to visit him at the Three Convolvuluses Farm. In 1924, he published *Cultivating the Soil and the Heart,* and went to the United States to investigate agriculture that same year. In 1935, he founded a school called the Cowshed at the Farm that provided students with an educational program of half-farming and

---

[2] These Latin terms are taken from Eto's own diagram of Agrayana Orbis Mandrus.

[3] Kimura Hiroshi, "The Wheel of Home Farming and Theory of Rural Reconstruction: Eto Tekirei and Liang Shuming," *Comparative Thought*, no. 26, March 2000, pp. 81-89.

half-study. His own children were taught at home and did not attend public schools, so this can be considered an early experiment in home schooling in modern Japan. Eto named the flower garden the HCS Garden, consisting of the initials of Home, Church, and School—reflecting his philosophy of combining family, faith, and education. Regarding his educational methods, some Japanese scholars have also compared them with Liang Shuming's ideas of "village education" and "rural education."[4] Although Liang Shuming visited Japan in 1936 to investigate the Rural Economic Revitalization Campaign, there is no record of any interaction with Eto.[5] The two may not have met, but in 1940 Eto received two

---

[4] Nishimura Shunichi, "Liang Shuming's Theory of Comparative Thought, and Educational Practice: A Comparative Study with Japanese Rural Educator Eto Tekirei," *International Education*, no. 21, March 2001, pp. 48-58.

[5] Liang Shuming's visit to Japan was the only time in his life that he went abroad. Regarding his visit to Japan, there are only records of two talks: "My Thoughts After Visiting Japan" and "Notes on Visiting the East." In them, he mentions that the only Japanese people he met were writer Hasegawa Nyozekan, *Nippon Hyoronsha* editor Murobuse Takanobu, Professor of Agriculture at Kyoto Imperial University Hashimoto Denzaemon, and Professor Koide Manji, an agronomist from Kyushu Imperial University. Chinese Academy of Culture eds., *Complete Works of Liang Shuming*, vol. 5 (Jinan: Shandong People's Publishing House, 1992), pp. 817-836.

Chinese visitors at the Three Convolvuluses Farm. One was Zhu Jinggu, who was then Director of the Shandong Education Department and had graduated from the Imperial University of Tokyo; he was also Liang Shuming's personal translator during his visit to Japan four years earlier. The other was Jiang Botang, whose name appears multiple times in Liang Shuming's journals. This is the only connection between Eto and Liang Shuming. Agriculturalism in China and Japan surged at the same time, and both eventually dissipated during the war.

The Heiminsha Farm had a brief existence, and the semi-agricultural lives of Tokutomi and Eto tended to be very personal, while the New Village and Kaributo Symbiotic Farm were more well-known collective utopian experiments. Due to their commitment to agricultural production in rural areas, involving a large number of people, and bold implementation of the communitarian system, they can be said to be fitting representatives of Japanese agricultural utopianism. Mushakoji was also an agriculturalist, and he was already considering Japan's agricultural issues when he conceived of New Village. Believing that modern methods should be used to manage agriculture, he said: "Organize a group of farmers to investigate the land in Japan, and plan the best way to use that land. Be equipped with modern tools, and use those tools regionally to build roads, as well as use trains and cars. Some can also use oxen and horses. Due to different climates, the order of cultivation and sowing should be determined, and the required number of people should be dispatched to various places according to the plan. In areas without water, large-scale wells can be dug to obtain a bottomless supply. When the sun is too strong, send people with modern equipment out in order to save some time. Doing this, the labor that farmers do for fifty years, even over their lifetimes, can be achieved in three or five years. All other times can be free."[6] Mushakoji believed that with new technologies, production efficiency could be improved, more leisure time could be created, art could be unleashed, and a fully developed "humane life" could be achieved. His agrarianism was not just a simple cliché about "building the nation through agriculture," but rather absorbed Tolstoy's theory

---

[6.] "Dialogue on the New Village," in *The New Village*, trans. Sun Baigang, p. 20.

of pan-laborism, viewing labor as "both a source of honor and grace," and leisure as a condition for freedom—and considering humanitarian happiness as the highest pursuit.[7] The inspiration for the autonomous mutual aid experiment of New Village came from Kropotkin, not from the East Asian political tradition of gentry autonomy under imperial power.

It is interesting that in the same year as the establishment of New Village at Kijo, the industrialist Kurosawa Teijiro, who invented the Katakana typewriter, built a 66,000-square-meter industrial utopia called Our Village in Kamata Village, Ebara, Tokyo. It contained workers' dormitories and farmland, and was also known as the Kurosawa Factory Village. It was considered a Japanese version of Robert Owen's New Lanark. In addition to Kurosawa Teijiro, textile tycoon Ohara Magosaburo worked towards workers' welfare reform and philanthropy, and the industrialist Teiichi Sakuma advocated the establishment of trade unions and the enactment of factory laws to protect workers' rights. They were also known as "the Owens of Japan,"

---

[7]. Ibid.

with the latter two enjoying a greater reputation than Kurosawa. According to publications in the village of New Lanark when I visited there, in the 1920s, the site received many Japanese visitors who were attracted by similarities in thinking and practice between historical Owenism and Japanese corporate culture at the time. Japan has the world's largest Robert Owen Research Association, and held a grand event in 1961 to commemorate the 103rd anniversary of his death.[8]

In 1926, Miyazawa Kenji, a poet and writer of fairy tales who remains deeply loved by Japanese people today, established the Rasuchijin Association in his hometown of Hanamaki, Iwate. At the time, he had just quit his teaching post at Hanamaki Agricultural High School and lived in the villa built by his grandfather Miyazawa Kisuke. While cultivating the earth, and growing vegetables and flowers, he held regular meetings with a group of young farmers about chemistry, soil science, botany, fertilizer science, "farmers' art," and Esperanto. He often traveled to promote fertilizer design, do agricultural consultations, and give talks about agriculture—

---

8. *The Story of New Lanark*, New Lanark Trust.

and he planned to organize a farmers' orchestra and a drama club, and helped them to host secondhand markets and seedling exchanges. Despite being harassed by the police, this small group, exploring agriculture, studying scientific agricultural technology, and developing farmers' art, continued for over two years. During the Showa period and under the fascist system, social movements began to be significantly restricted. In that situation, the anarchist Ishikawa Sanshiro quietly rented a quarter-hectare of land in Funabashi, Chitose, and renovated a village house there. In 1927, he established the Kyougakusha (Mutual Learning Association). Before, Chitose had Tokutomi Kenjiro and Eto Tekirei there, but later it had Ishikawa. It seems to have become a popular place for intellectuals to go back to the land. There were around 20 anarchists who followed Ishikawa, and together they planted apple trees and various crops, raised livestock such as chickens, pigs, sheep, and rabbits, and were self-sufficient. At the same time, they published and distributed *Force* magazine and various books to promote their ideas.

Subsequently, in 1928, Okamoto Rikichi purchased 40 hectares of mountain forest and built 13 houses in Tomioka Village, Shizuoka (now Susono), establishing the Rural Youth Cooperative School. Okamoto had previously engaged in social activism in Tokyo. In 1919, he established the Constitutional Enterprise Association, and in 1920, he founded Kameido Cooperative, which expanded throughout the Kanto region. The Rural Youth Cooperative School, founded on the hillside of Mount Ashitaka, near the southern foot of Mount Fuji, lasted for six years. More than 100 students from all over Japan worked on land reclamation, planting crops such as rice, wheat, and sweet potatoes. They attended culture classes in the morning and worked in the afternoon, leading self-sufficient lives. They also opened the Pure Society Canteen for workers in Shitamachi, Tokyo. In 1929, Tachibana Kozaburo launched the Love Your Homeland Association and established branches in multiple regions. In 1931, he established a branch in his hometown of Joban Village (now Mito City) in Ibaraki, and established a rural school called Love Your Homeland School—a practice site for the Love Your Homeland Association and to promote "Love-Your-Homelandism," cultivating "warriors for the construction of New Japan." In his early years, Tachibana was familiar with the works of Kropotkin and Osugi Sakae, and was also influenced by Tolstoy, the White Birch Society, and Kang Youwei. As early as 1915, he attempted to run a "brotherhood farm," and had a confidante in Inoue Nissho, who organized the Blood Oath group (Ketsumeidan) that assassinated Grand Minister Inoue Junnosuke. Tachibana also wrote five volumes of *On the Emperor*. In the aftermath of the May 15th Incident of 1932, during which Navy Lieutenant Koga Kiyoshi assassinated Inukai Tsuyoshi, Tachibana organized the Farmer Death Squad and led seven students from his school to attack a substation in Tokyo. He was sentenced to life imprisonment, and the Love Your Homeland School was subsequently disbanded in 1933. Gondo Seikyo was also imprisoned for spreading his ideas, but was later acquitted and released.

In the return to agriculture trend of the early Showa period, Miyazawa Kenji did not have clear political inclinations. Ishikawa Sanshiro was a left-wing figure, Tachibana Kozaburo was an extreme right-wing figure, and Okamoto Rikichi was a left-wing figure in his early period and later became a right-wing figure. After experiencing the revival and decline of social movements during the Taisho era, Japanese intellectuals, regardless of where they were on the political spectrum, remained consistent about returning to agriculture. Before the Rural Economic Revitalization Campaign and the Imperial Rural Establishment Campaign, to promote local improvements and stimulate the vitality of agriculture and fishing, the Home Ministry organized village governance surveys and model village elections throughout Japan. Inatori, one of the three model villages in Shizuoka Prefecture, was praised as a "socialist village" by Katayama Sen. To save rural areas, many socialists began to "turn around" and support the government-led "town and village autonomy" policy.[9] Although Ishikawa was agriculturally-oriented, he opposed the intrusion of nationalism into rural areas.

Although Ishikawa's Kyougakusha was small in scale, he had great influence through his writings. Kato Kazuo read Ishikawa's books and believed

---

[9]. See Nishiyama Taku, "Utopianism in the Thought and Action of Ishikawa Sanshiro."

that coexistence with nature was the only authentic life, and he began his own semi-agricultural life. In the process of writing the *Theory of the Farmer's Art*, Miyazawa Kenji referred to Ishikawa's "On Non-Evolution and Life." Tachibana Kozaburo was also influenced by Ishikawa's discourses on Agricultural Fundamentalism.[10] When Ishikawa Sanshiro was young, he was baptized a Christian. After graduating from Tokyo Law School, he joined the *Yorozu Choho* newspaper and worked with Kotoku Shusui, Sakai Toshihiko, and Uchimura Kanzo, eventually becoming a socialist. Later, he joined the Heiminsha and published the newspaper *Heimin Shinbun (Civic News)*, which was banned after it published a translation of *The Communist Manifesto*. Later still, he wrote *A History of Japanese Socialism*. In 1910, he was implicated in the High Treason Incident, and fled to Europe after the death of Kotoku Shusui. After the killing of Osugi Sakae in 1923, he became the core figure in Japanese anarchism. The reason he decided to return to agriculture was related to his experience of Edward Carpenter's life of farming in England, and living with anarchists in the countryside for six

---

10. Ibid.

years in France: "All inauthentic and illusory lives were completely overturned, and authentic human life made me see that there was nothing stronger than farmers."[11] His Agricultural Fundamentalism was reflected in treating farmers as the most important revolutionary force.

He felt "very happy" about the popularity of Agricultural Fundamentalism, but he preferred to explore his own "earthmen thought." In his view, "agriculture is the foundation of the nation" only demonstrated a rulers' patrimony. So-called "town and village autonomy" was mechanically organized, while true autonomy was organic and could only be earthed, relying on earthmen to achieve it.[12] The term "earthmen"(*domin*) had previously been an insulting term, referring to those who had subsistence-level existences. It was not limited to farmers, but any who "participated in the great art of heaven and earth:" "Like the utopian socialism of

---

[11]. Ishikawa Sanshiro, "Before Entering the Half-Agricultural Life," *Yomiuri Shimbun*, March 21, 1927. Aozora Library: https://www.aozora.gr.jp/

[12]. Ishikawa Sanshiro, "Agricultural Fundamentalism and Earthmen Thought," *Force*, September 1, 1932. Aozora Library: https://www.aozora.gr.jp/

a hundred years prior, Agricultural Fundamentalism aims to achieve conflict-free development under the existing class system."[13] Agricultural Fundamentalism may appease people under the current system, but "that is not liberation. The earthmen thought cannot develop without class struggle. Earthmen must first cut themselves free from barbed wire before they can unite, work together, and gain freedom."[14] In 1945, when the Showa Emperor announced his surrender, Ishikawa organized the Japanese Anarchist Alliance, and wrote the *Anarchist Declaration*, showing the determination to build an anarchist society in the post-war peaceful environment. His anti-war attitude was not sudden, but his sympathy and support for the Showa Emperor surprised many leftists and anarchists.

---

13. Ibid.
14. Ibid.

The restored building of Rasuchijin Association is located on the campus of the Hanamaki Agricultural High School, with a chalkboard hanging at the entrance in the style of Miyazawa Kenji's handwriting that reads: "I am in the field below."

Photo by Ou Ning, 2019.

THE IHATOV

Miyazawa Kenji was one of the literary geniuses of the late Taisho and early Showa periods. His brief life was not tarnished by politics, and he left behind a literary legacy that has continued to attract people to his hometown. Hanamaki is located in the northeast interior of Japan, west of the center of Iwate County, and in the middle of Kitakami Valley. It is traditionally an agricultural area. Today, the Miyazawa Kenji Museum, the Miyazawa Kenji Society, Miyazawa Kenji Forest, Miyazawa Kenji Dowa Mura (Village of Fairy Tales), Miyazawa Kenji's birth home, his grave, and the restored building of the Rasuchijin Association are available for visitors to visit and pay their respects. Many restaurants and cafes use his works in their names, and his poems are ubiquitous. This poet, writer of fairy tales, Buddhist, naturalist, agronomist, and utopian dreamer is the signature of the tourism industry here.

I came here to explore the Ihatov of Miyazawa's literary universe, a utopia completely different from Mushakoji Saneatsu's New Village. The museum is located on the high slope of a hill forest around seven kilometers east of Hanamaki Railway Station. This area is called the Miyazawa Kenji Forest (the English on the tour signboard says Ihatov Forest). Mysterious Ihatov has obviously been turned into an artificial reality by the tourism industry. In addition to the museum, there is also the Miyazawa Kenji Society at the foot of the hill—and the building where the society is has another name, the Miyazawa Kenji Ihatov Center. Going east on National Highway 456 from the Miyazawa Kenji Society will be Miyazawa Kenji Dowa Mura, a theme park aimed at parent-child entertainment.

The restored building of Rasuchijin Association is located on the campus of the Hanamaki Agricultural High School (where Miyazawa once taught), near Hanamaki Airport. Surrounding the building is a courtyard. On the grass, there is a standing statue of him, bowed with his head in thought, as well as a poem of his—the Hanamaki Agricultural High School Anthem. The restored building is in Minka style of Meiji period, with a chalkboard hanging at the entrance in the style of his handwriting that reads: "I am in the field below." This famous phrase of his in chalk vividly shows Miyazawa's devotion to farming. The interior of the building is decorated with furniture according to how the Rasuchijin Association gathered in the past, and some historical photos are hung on the walls. There are neither guards nor tourists, though a festival is held every September 21st to commemorate his birthday.

There are many scholarly interpretations of the name *rasu chijin kyokai* (in English, The Society of Rasu Earthmen, or the Rasuchijin Association). *Chijin* refers to farmers, and carries a meaning similar to Ishikawa Sanshiro's use of the term *domin*. This is fairly easy to see, but then what does *rasu* mean? Up to the time of his death, Miyazawa never gave any specific explanation. He only said that *rasu* had no special meaning—just like Hanamaki, it was only a name. Some have said that, in Japanese, *rasu* is *asura* read backwards—as it is "non-asuras" that are the Pure Land. Some people say that, in Japanese, *ra* refers to the "four dimensions" (of the world), and that *su* is an accented word for "need to wait"—altogether meaning "the world needs to wait (for the Rasu Earthmen)." And some have said that Miyazawa was quoting William Morris when he was teaching *Theory of the Farmer's Art*—Morris and John Ruskin were important figures in the Arts and Crafts Movement—with *rasu* being a Japanese homophone for "Ruskin." Some have further said that *rasu* is a homophone for "lath" in English, indicating that earthmen are indeed the "pillars" of the world. Miyazawa liked to create new words, and his poetry and fairy tales contain a large number of similarly new words, giving readers and translators plenty to argue about and ponder.

Though few, his original manuscripts, publications, photos, and daily necessities have been collected at the Miyazawa Kenji Museum. The exhibition in the museum is divided into five parts, based on the major themes in his life—

agriculture, religion, the universe, art, and science. Due to the small number of objects, new exhibition design methods across media are used to expand the content, and fill an exhibition hall that is disproportionate to the size of the collection. This is similar to the approach of other Miyazawa sites. I bought a booklet of *Outline of the Theory of the Farmer's Art* there. The 1926 outline, used for instruction at the Rasuchijin Association, is only 2500 words, and even with a chronicle of Miyazawa's life as an appendix it is only 28 pages long. But it gives a glimpse into his thoughts on agriculturalism.

"We are all farmers, working tirelessly towards a brighter and more vibrant way of life," he begins. "There can be no individual happiness until the world reaches complete happiness. Self-consciousness gradually evolves from individual to collective, to society, to the universe. Isn't this the path of enlightenment that the ancient sages followed?" Integrating individuals into the community and the world was precisely the purpose of his association. Then, "Why advocate our art now? Although our ancestors were poor, they lived happy and contented lives. Then, they had both art and religion, but now we only strive for survival through labor... Today, we must take the right path, create our own beauty, and use art to ignite the spark in the dimness of our labor." What then is the essence of the farmer's art? "Beauty is the essence... The farmer's art is a manifestation of the connection between the characters of earthmen and the emotions of the universe... always affirming, deepening, and improving actual life." He then writes about classifications, styles, the creative process, and interaction between creativity and criticism in the farmer's art, finally calling on all people to work together, "to create a magnificent four-dimensional art from all our fields and all our lives, that soars into the sky and becomes the dust of the universe scattered in the boundless void." To accomplish this feat, it was necessary to have "the thorough determination to surround the Milky Way" and "powerful will and energy." Also: "The road ahead is both glorious and steep, but every difficulty is an improvement in the scale and depth of our four-dimensional art. Poets enjoy this hardship the most, because the eternal unfinished is what is called completion."[1] This last sentence best reflects his utopian spirit.

This utopian spirit is in imagining a beautiful place, knowing that it does not exist in the real world, yet still exploring it and enjoying its continuous exploration. Miyazawa's utopia, Ihatov, only exists in literature and is a fictional place name—not a practice. However, when he publicly disclosed the secrets of his writing, it was actually related to reality. Ihatov first appeared in the 1923 poetry collection *Ihatov's Icy Mist,* and in the fairy tale "Fur of the Ice River Mouse" (about "people departing from Ihatov on a train and heading towards Bering at 8pm on December 26," published in the *Iwate Daily News*). It also appeared in the book of fairy tales, *The Adventures of the Tax Commissioner,* and the poetry collection *Summer Fantasy,* in the same year. In 1924, the term appeared multiple times in the poetry collection *Spring and Asura.* According to Yonechi Fumio, "Ihatov" and its derived place names appear in a total of 30 fairy tales and poems by Miyazawa

---

[1] Miyazawa Kenji, *Outline of the Theory of the Farmers' Art* (Hanamaki: Hanamaki Cultural Group Council, 2018).

Kenji.[2] From the suffix of the term, it looks like somewhere in Russia. It sometimes becomes "Ihatovo," which looks like a noun in Esperanto.[3] Beginning with "I," it is the same as the Romanized spelling of "Iwate." Replacing real Japanese place names with made-up foreign spellings and then using them as fictional place names is very common in Miyazawa's work.

The only collection of fairy tales he published during his lifetime was *The Restaurant with Many Orders,* published in 1924 by Toryo Shuppanbu and Tokyo Kogensha. The promotional advertisement for the book was personally written by him, and it is also the only text in which he himself explains Ihatov: "Ihatov is a place name. If you have to say where it is, the fields cultivated by Little Claus and Big Claus, as well as the looking-glass world experienced by the

---

[2] Yonechi Fumio, "A Geographical Study of the Origin and Changes in the Toponym 'Ihatov' Created by Miyazawa Kenji," *Annual Journal of the Iwate University Faculty of Education,* vol. 55, no. 2, 1996, pp. 45-64.

[3] Esperanto, invented by Polish doctor L. L. Zamenhof in 1887, was, after World War I, considered a utopian language that could potentially transcend geography and race. It once sparked interest in Arishima Takeo, Mushakoji Saneatsu, and Zhou Zuoren. Miyazawa Kenji not only studied Esperanto himself, but also taught Esperanto at the Rasuchijin Association.

young girl Alice, are all located within it. It is located in the far northeast of the desert of Tepantar, east of Ivan's Kingdom. In fact, it is the Iwate Prefecture of Japan that exists in the author's mind, in a lifelike dream. There, anything is possible. A person can jump over the ice and clouds in an instant, ride on the air current northward, or talk to ants under a red flowerpot. There, even sin and sorrow shine with a divine and a loving light. The deep beech forest, wind and shadow, evening primrose, the wonderful city, and rows of light pillars extend all the way to Bering City: it is a truly mysterious and happy country."[4] In this passage, "Little Claus and Big Claus" comes from a fairytale by Hans Christian Andersen; "Alice" comes from Lewis Carroll's *Alice in Wonderland*; the "desert of Tepantar" comes from Rabindranath Tagore's poem "Land of Exile;" "Ivan's Kingdom" comes from Leo Tolstoy's fairy tale "Ivan the Fool;" and Bering City is a city created by Miyazawa based on the Bering Strait as the "land of the far north."

His utopia was, in reality, Iwate. Ihatov Town

---

[4] Miyazawa Kenji, "New Publication Information for *The Restaurant of Many Orders*," in Amazawa Taijiro, *Photo Collection: The World of Miyazawa Kenji* (Tokyo: Chikuma Shobo, 1996), p. 76.

is Hanamaki, the Ihatov River is the Kitakami River that flows through Hanamaki, the Ihatov Volcano is Iwate Mountain, the Ihatov Coast is the inland coast Rikuchu Kaigan in the east of Iwate County, and Ihatov City is Morioka, the capital of Iwate, where from 1909 to 1920 he went to high school, studied agriculture, and did graduate work. When the mysteries of geography are revealed, the Rasuchijin Association can naturally be understood as the practical version of Ihatov. It was not a utopian escape from the Tokyo metropolitan area to a remote rural area, as with Mushakoji Saneatsu, as it was already rooted in an agricultural region. Its "farmers' art" was not the leisure activity of urban intellectuals, but rather what the farmers themselves required and wanted for their cultural life. From these two points of view, the Rasuchijin Association may be more like Wang Gongbi's village autonomy and rural reconstruction experiment in his hometown of Xiaowuying Village. Miyazawa's agricultural thinking has much to do with his study of agriculture in Morioka, and his teaching at the Hanamaki Agricultural High School. He loved nature and lived a simple life, "eating half a liter of black rice with *miso* and a few vegetables every day."[5.] He enjoyed hiking off to do fieldwork, studying the soil, minerals, fertilizer, and farming, forming groups with farmers, advocating mutual aid, opposing competition, writing poems in praise of the countryside, and writing fairy tales for children. In order to organize a farmers' art troupe, he even taught himself the cello. He devoted himself wholeheartedly to the construction of this agricultural utopia, but unfortunately passed away at the age of 37.

Fortunately, it was precisely because of his early death that he was able to avoid the taint of politics, and not be absorbed into extreme nationalism. In 1933, when he passed away, Agricultural Fundamentalism and Pan-Asianism had been introduced into official ideology for war mobilization, and, following the trajectory of his thought, he had already encountered the allure of Japanese fascism. Miyazawa originally followed his father, Miyazawa Masajiro, in believing in Pure Land Buddhism. But in 1914, at the age of 18, he studied a Chinese-

---

5. Miyazawa Kenji's 1931 poem "Rain Won't", illustrated edition in Japanese, English, and Chinese, trans. Cheng Bi (Beijing: United Publishing Company, 2016).

Japanese version of the *Lotus Sutra*, which jolted him into following the Hokkeshu sect of Buddhism. Eventually, in 1920, he converted to Nichiren Buddhism and joined the Nichiren organization, Kokuchukai. Because of that, he and his father had a falling out, and he left home in January 1921 to move to Tokyo. There, he met with the director of the Kokuchukai, Takachio Chiyo, and began preaching on the street. Tanaka Chigaku, the founder of the Kokuchukai, along with Inoue Nissho, were both members of Nichiren. Along with the fascist theorist Kita Ikki and the militarist Ishiwara Kanji, they represented the extreme nationalism of the time. But Miyazawa stuck to reading his copy of *The Doctrine of the Japanese Lotus Sages* and *The Lecture Notes of Myoshu*. In August, he returned to Hanamaki because his sister was ill, and was able to remain far from the influence of the Kokuchukai in Tokyo. Today, many of the scholars who admire Miyazawa have tried to sever the relationship between Miyazawa and the Kokuchukai. However, some believe that his belief in Hokkeshu did lead him to practice vegetarianism and environmentalism—setting his utopian actions apart from the semi-agricultural lifestyles of Japanese intellectuals during the same period, and even influencing today's deep ecology movement. So, there is no need to avoid recognizing his relationship to Kokuchukai. After all, Hokkeshu itself is not nationalist, it was only politically exploited.[6]

---

[6] This paper analyzes the utopian world of Miyazawa Kenji from the perspective of Hokkeshu: Melissa Anne-Marie Curley, "Fruit, Fossils, Footprints: Cathecting Utopia in the Work of Miyazawa Kenji", in Daniel Boscaljon ed., *Hope and the Longing for Utopia: Futures and Illusions in Theology and Narrative* (Eugene: Pickwick Publications, 2014), pp. 96-118.

The statue of Ando Shoeki in front of the Ando Shoeki Museum, Hachinohe.
Photo by Ou Ning, 2019.

PATRON SAINT OF AGRICULTURE

North of the inland coast of Iwate is the Tanesashi Coast of Aomori. These two coastlines, along with Oshika Hanto Coast in southern Miyagi, are collectively known as the Sanriku Coast. Rocks, beaches, and rusted platforms form a jagged curve that stretches over 600 kilometers, geologically known as the Rias coastal terrain. In 1933, the Showa Sanriku Tsunami occurred here, causing a massive disaster in the northeastern and Pacific coastal areas. It added salt to wounds that had not yet healed from the agricultural panic of 1930-1931. At first glance, I thought the area was a golf course, with vast, open, and undulating natural grasslands across the

Tanesashi Coast, with rocks that had been pounded by waves. Climbing onto the Ashigezaki Observatory, one can look out over the reeds and reefs onto the endless Pacific Ocean. Further north, there is a vast and dense pine forest, with no signs of humanity in sight. In the primitive forest, the paths of moist soil are winding, and secluded. Through gaps between vigorous old pine trees, the ocean is still visible. Put in two or three travelers and their porters from the Edo period, and it would be a typical Ukiyo-e print by Utagawa Hiroshige. On November 10th to 12th, 1971, Shiba Ryotaro was here. He wrote in the *Asahi Weekly*: "If aliens ever come to earth, this is the place I most want to show them."[1] Why did Shiba Ryotaro come to the Tanesashi Coast? Because the city on the shore, Hachinohe, is where a philosopher from the Edo period, Ando Shoeki, once lived.

Ando Shoeki first entered the purview of modern Japanese intellectuals in the late Meiji period. In 1899, Kano Kokichi, who was born in Odate, Akita, and served as Principal of The First Higher School, discovered by chance a manuscript

---

[1]. Shiba Ryotaro, "Matsu no Kuni," and "A Walk Down the Street" (Asahi bunko, 1978).

entitled *Shizen shin'eido* (*The True Way of Administering According to Nature*) at a used bookstore in Tokyo, consisting of 100 volumes of 92 books, plus the *Great Introduction*—in total making 101 volumes of 93 books. The author was "Fujiwara Ryoutyuu of Kakuryudo." Kano learned from the book collector Utida of Tensyoudou that the original holder of the manuscript was Hasimoto Rituzou, from the end of the Edo and the early Meiji period, and the author was Ando Shoeki, who was born in Odate in the middle of the Edo period, and had previously practiced medicine in Hachinohe, Akita. After reading through the manuscript written by his fellow townsman, he was shocked by the advanced and radical ideas, and called it "the book of a madman." Due to concerns that Ando's ideas would be too controversial, using the name "Doctor of Literature," Kano Kokichi wrote an article entitled "The Thinker" for the January 8, 1908 issue of *Education Review*, published through his connections to journalist Kiyama Kumazi, in which he publicly discussed his findings. Shortly afterwards, on the 24th of the same month, *Heimin Shinbun*, founded by Kotoku Shusui, published an article entitled "An Anarchist from

150 Years Ago: Ando Shoeki" (author anonymous), spreading the discovery. Eto Tekirei had begun reading Ando Shoeki in 1925, while Kano Kokichi did not publish his essay, "Ando Shoeki," under his real name in *World Currents* magazine (published by Iwanami Shoten) until May 1928—calling him an "agrarian communist" and "possibly the only great thinker Japan can boast about to the world."[2]

Kano had been the first president of the College of Letters at Kyoto Imperial University from 1906 to 1907, and obtained a doctoral degree in literature after one year in office. He became regarded as a person with dangerous ideas for promoting Ando. He resigned from his position in 1907 and began to make a living by collecting and identifying ancient books and paintings in 1923, becoming the

---

[2]. Information about the discovery of Ando Shoeki by Kano Kokichi, and Shoeki's books, is from: Yasunaga Toshinobu ed., photography by Yamada Hukuo, *Photobook: Ando Shoeki* (Tokyo: Rural Culture Association Japan, 1987), pp. 114-116; Wang Shouhua ed., *Ando Shoeki Research Material Index* (Department of Philosophy, Shandong University, 1985); Wang Shouhua, "Ando Shoeki and *Shizen shin'eido*," and Li Jinshan,"Re-Exploring of the Significance of the Discovery Ando Shoeki discovered by Kano Kokichi," in Wang Shouhua and Li Caihua, eds., *Ando Shoeki · Modern · China: Collection of the Sino-Japanese Ando Shoeki Academic Symposium* (Jinan: Shandong People's Publishing House, 1993), pp. 27-28; pp. 220-221.

largest collector of Japanese ukiyo-e and shunga paintings at the time. In March of that year, due to financial constraints, he sold the manuscript of *Shizen shin'eido* to the Imperial Tokyo University for two thousand yen (which was a huge sum at the time—Mushakoji Saneatsu got five thousand yen for selling a house in Abiko). Six months later, in September, a major earthquake occurred in Kanto. Except for twelve books that happened to be checked out at the time, all others were destroyed by the fire after the earthquake. The surviving twelve volumes include the *Great Introduction*, which allowed for the preservation of the complete manuscript's table of contents and a full outline of its ideas. Later, Kano found three more books from the manuscript in used bookstores, bringing the total to fifteen existing books. Later on, three volumes of *Shizen shin'eido,* published by Ando in Kyoto, were discovered. Today scholars refer to these three volumes as "publications," "small versions," and "small books"—and refer to the one hundred and one volumes of Ando's handwritten works as "manuscripts," "large versions," and "large books." Fragments and publications of *Shizen shin'eido*, as well as another five-volume manuscript discovered by Kano in 1925, *Todo shinden* (*A True Account of the Transmission of the Way*), were successively compiled and published by the Rural Culture Association Japan in 1982 as the *Complete Collection of Ando Shoeki*.

Ando Shoeki was born in 1703 into a landholding family in Niida Village, Dewa Province (now Odate, in Akita). In his early years, he went to the Myoshinji Temple in Kyoto to practice Zen and also visited the Kitano Tenmangu Shrine, to make offerings to the Shinto god of learning Sugawara no Michizane. However, he later became skeptical of Buddhism and Shinto, and decided to switch his focus to medicine and herbology. In 1744, he left Niida with his family and began practicing medicine in Jusannichi, Hachinohe, Mutsu Province. In 1746, in order to avoid Catholic persecution by the Tokugawa shogunate, he was registered at the Pure Land Ganei Temple. Although his name appears in the temple's account books, it was not his true faith. In 1752 he began writing *Todo shinden* and *Shizen shin'eido*. In 1753, *Shizen shin'eido* was published, and then reprinted the following year. From then on, he continued to expand the book. In 1757, his disciples gathered at the Tenshoji Temple in Hachinohe for a lecture and discussion. In 1758, after the death of his older brother, he left his wife and son, who was already able to practice medicine independently in Hachinohe, and returned alone to Niida Village to take on the family business. In 1760, 14 disciples from Matsumae, Kyoto, and Osaka went to Niida for a lecture and discussion, the record of which was later included in the 25th volume of *Shizen shin'eido*, as *Symposium*. The *Great Introduction* was written last, but before finishing Ando passed away, in 1762 due to illness.

The *Great Introduction* was completed by Ando's disciple Kamiyama Senakira, based on oral records. In the last four years of his tenure in Niida Village, Ando was treating villagers while promoting the "Right Cultivation" idea of *Shizen shin'eido*. Under the influence of his atheistic beliefs, farmers stopped worshipping the gods. On the second anniversary of his death, villagers erected a memorial stele for him in Niida Village, calling him the "Patron Saint of Agriculture." Later scholars also praised him highly. Canadian scholar of Japanese E. H. Norman published *Ando Shoeki and the Anatomy of Japanese Feudalism* in 1949, calling him "the first person to criticize Japanese feudal society."[3] In his book *History of Philosophy*, Yakov Radul-Zatulovsky of the Soviet Union referred to him as "a materialist, a fighting atheist, and the earliest utopian socialist in history."[4] The translator of his English-language collection, Yasunaga Toshinobu, referred to him as an "encyclopedic intellectual."[5] Social activist and writer Iida Momo refers to his thought as "dialectics before Hegel, communism before Marx, ecology before Haeckel, and the pioneer of the critique of Confucianism before Lu Xun."[6] He has been included in Japanese primary and secondary school textbooks, and has been included in histories of world philosophy, being discussed at various international philosophy conferences. In 1990, NHK produced a large-scale historical documentary film on him, *Revolutionary Thought in the Age of Genroku: On the Trail of Ando Shoeki*.

---

[3] E. H. Norman, *Ando Shoeki and the Anatomy of Japanese Feudalism* (Tokyo: The Asiatic Society of Japan, 1949).

[4] Yakov Radul-Zatulovsky, "Ando Shoeki," *History of Philosophy Vol. 1* (Beijing: Sanlian, 1959).

[5] *Photobook: Ando Shoeki,* p. 35. The English translation of Ando's work is *Ando Shoeki: Social and Ecological Philosopher in Eighteenth-Century Japan* (New York: Weatherhill, 1992).

[6] Iida Momo, "Ando Shoeki: Critic of Zhu Xi" in *Ando Shoeki ·Modern ·China: Collection of the Sino-Japanese Ando Shoeki Academic Symposium*, p. 177.

The small commemorative pillar placed on the approximate location of Ando Shoeki's former residence in Jusannichi, Hachinohe.
Photo by Ou Ning, 2019.

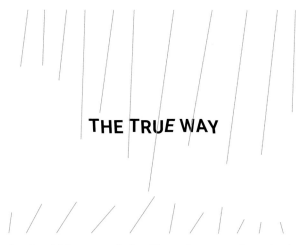

THE TRUE WAY

In the 16th year of the Genroku era, when Ando was born, the population of Japan increased from 10 million in the early Edo period to 30 million, and the demand for food due to population growth promoted the development of agriculture. The Genroku era (1688-1704) was a period of rapid growth in the rice farming society of Japan, and rice cultivation expanded to the cold northeastern region. At the same time, the trade relationship between China and Japan, formed after the lifting of a Ming Dynasty maritime ban, continued, further promoting the development of commerce in Japan. China's massive demand for Japanese precious metals (gold, silver, and copper—the "three goods" used for minting currency) led to a boom in mining and exports from Japan, making Nagasaki a bustling port. The activities of *chonin* (townsmen)[1] led to the proliferation of brothels and casinos, making Edo a den of spending that attracted the envy of visiting foreigners. After Ando moved to Hachinohe, the Edo shogunate took control of the export of silver and copper, replacing it with *tawaramono* (dried marine products) to meet the Qing dynasty demand for palace delicacies. This led to the emergence of fishing tycoons operating shark fin and abalone exports in Nagasaki from the Sanriku Coast. During the reign of Emperor Qianlong, soybeans became popular among Chinese. They could not only be pressed into edible oil, lamp oil, and furniture coating, but the dregs could be used as fertilizer. In Japan, it was the raw material of soy sauce that people ate with every meal. Under the encouragement and reward of the shogunate, the northeastern regions, which had never produced soybeans, also began to cultivate them. Due to the low soil fertility, cultivation required the burn-off land, which then had to rest between

---

1. General terms for the urban business class during the Edo period.

rotations. This attracted wild boars which fed and bred in large numbers, and in turn consumed all the crops in both fallow and active farmland. This led to the Wild Boar Famine of 1749, which resulted in the deaths of more than three thousand people. In addition, the climate of the northeast is harsh, with inclement winds, snows, and floods. In 1744, 1747, and 1755, a total of three natural disasters occurred in Hachinohe, resulting in a total of 42,000 *dan*[2] of food loss and five thousand deaths from starvation.[3] It was during this unrelenting "time of evil and disaster" that Ando transformed from a doctor who diagnosed and treated human physical diseases to a utopian dreamer who criticized the times and tried to improve society, creating his own vast and complex system.

Today, the General Library of University of Tokyo has turned the surviving manuscript of

---

2. *dan*, an ancient unit of volume in China and Japan, was usually used to measure rice. In Edo period of Japan, 1 *dan* was 52.5 kilograms of rice.
3. The above historical facts are based on articles by Sakamoto Syou, Wang Shouhua, and Iida Momo in *Ando Shoeki · Modern · China: Collection of the Sino-Japanese Ando Shoeki Academic Symposium*; "Ando Shoeki Chronology and Related Historical Events" in *Photobook: Ando Shoeki*; as well as Ueda Shin, *The Sea and Empire: Ming and Qing Dynasties*, tr. Gao Yingying (Guilin: Guangxi Normal University Press, 2014).

Shizen shin'eido into a public resource by uploading a facsimile of the twelve volumes, page after page, onto its website. The entire book is written in a variant of Classical Chinese. As can be seen from the table of contents in the *Great Introduction*, the manuscript of *Shizen shin'eido* is divided into two sections. The first section consists of "General Studies" and "Merits and Demerits in Ancient Teachings." It critiques previous thought, including Confucianism, Buddhism, phonetics, Shinto codes, the circulation of energy and the calendar, medical texts, and the *Book of Changes*. It also includes dialogues with Confucians, military strategists, doctors, Buddhists, Daoists, and Shintoists. Along with "Tales of the World of Law" it totals twenty-four volumes. The second section is the argument of *Shizen shin'eido*, consisting of seventy-six volumes. The twenty-fifth volume, *Symposium*, was considered by Ando to be "the torch to see" the book with. The following sections expand on these themes: "The Mutual Nature of the Circulation of the Energy of Heaven-and-Earth, the Subtle Way of the Living Truth;" "The Production of Grain Through the Circulation of Energy;" "The Production of Man-

and-Woman (the person) from Grain;" "The Self-Acting World;" "Knowing the Interior Workings of Human Beings by Observing Their Faces;" "On Life and Death;" "On the Lives of the Sages, Shakyamuni, and Prince Shotoku;" "How Heaven-and-Earth and Man-and-Woman are two aspects of the Same Existence;" "The Circulation of Energy in All Things;" "The Circulation of Energy in All Lands;" "Errors in the Ancient Methods of Medicine;" "On the Illness of Heaven-and-Earth;" "Notes on the Properties of Medicines;" "The Subtle Activity of Energy;" and "Various Symptoms of Illness." They are accompanied by three impressive volumes of illustrations.

Under the influence of the Chinese culture brought back by envoys to Sui and Tang, Ando became familiar with the Chinese classics and eventually became their fervent opponent. He wrote in his *Great Introduction*: "All letters are nothing more than arbitrary and capricious constructions contrived by the sages of old. They use characters to make study with books, and use that to place themselves above all others, and with the excuse that they were going to teach those below them, they established self-serving laws. Then they were able to eat greedily without cultivating and thieved Heaven's Way of Right Cultivation. Saying that they were 'pacifying the realm,' they planted the roots of thievery and strife. From that time on, forever and ever, the world has been one of thievery and strife. We can see, then, that books and learning are merely tools to thieve Heaven's Way. Those who make characters and learning were in ignorance of the fact that the Way of Living Truth is apparent in the hearth and human face. Those who employ characters and learning with books are the great foes of Heaven's Truth. This is the reason that I do not make use of characters and learning with books."[4] The term "Heaven-and-Earth" is composed of the characters 转 (to rotate) and 定 (to fix). He uses them idiosyncratically, as if they were synonymous with heaven (天) and earth (地). He regarded intellectuals as parasites who were physically unable to engage in farming, who did not participate in it, and knew nothing about it. He also regarded their works as the root cause of social

---

4. Toshinobu Yasunaga, *Ando Shoeki: Social and Ecological Philosopher in Eighteenth Century Japan* (New York: Weatherhill, 1992), *The Great Introduction*, p. 268.

inequality and the turbulence caused by bad laws and personal greed: "Confucians, Buddhists, Daoists, Shintoists—all of their books are like this," without exception, he wrote. "Sages have fractured the world, and Shakyamuni fractured our minds." Without any fear of violating taboos or slandering the sages, he continued: "A certain person asked me, 'When you say that Heaven-and-Earth are a single body and man-and-woman are one person, that there is no dualism between ruler and ruled, noble and humble, good and evil, you seem to be slandering the sages and Shakyamuni and full of self-conceit. Is that so?' I replied, '…The sages established the self-serving laws of a dualism between ruler and ruled because in their unbalanced knowledge they were ignorant of the Way of the Truth of mutualization of natures. What need could there be to slander such as these?' My questioner foamed at the mouth and left."[5] In the context of the Edo shogunate ruling Japan through Zhu Xi's Neo-Confucianism as the official school, this not only deviated from the norm, but was subversive.

After criticizing Confucianism, Buddhism,

---

[5] Ibid., *The Great Introduction*, pp. 272-273.

Laozi, Zhuangzi, Shinto, and doctors, one by one, in *Tales of the World of Law* he includes the World of Birds, the World of Beasts, the World of Crawling Creatures, and the World of Fish. He believed that these worlds were essentially the same as the World of Law that humans formed through the historical accumulation of philosophies and Shinto codes, and all followed the competition and exploitation of big-eat-small: "The Eagle, which of all birds has the strongest advancing energy, is our ruler. The Crane is our court noble, our great lord steward; the Hawk, our feudal lord; the Crow, our craftsman; the Magpie, our merchant; the Buzzard-Eagle, our master; and all the smaller birds are their servants."[6] The feudal hierarchical system and the ordering of the "four ranks"—of scholars, farmers, workers, and merchants—in the World of Law were no different from the World of Birds. Regarding cultural inheritance, from Fuxi to Confucius, from the Cheng brothers to Zhu Xi, from Tang, Song, and Ming literature to Sorai's teaching, "all literary studies and criticism are nothing but the peeping of birds." When "rites and music" spread to Japan, "men pluck

---

6. Ibid., *Tales of the World of Law*, pp. 119-120.

the samisen, koto, and zither[7] while, following the Mandarin Duck's lead, they lose their head in lust and drink," and "men take to gambling, and gambling leads to arson and thievery. Thus it is that every activity of the human World of Law finds its model in the World of Birds."[8] His conclusion was that "all because of the use of gold and silver currency in the human World of Law, there is no end to lust and delusion, thievery and revolt."[9] This is probably how he actually felt about his times; the indulgences of money in Edo showed an unequal and crazed society, and the human tragedy of the Wild Boar Famine exposed the shogunate's greed in agriculture and ignorance of natural ecology. He explained nature and human society from the perspective of the food chain, a century prior to Charles Darwin's theory of evolution and of the survival of the fittest, as proposed in *The Origin of Species* in 1859.

Faced with the World of Law, Ando denied all the ancient thought he had studied, and the alternative theory he developed was the "true way

---

7. All are traditional Japanese instruments originating from China.
8. Ibid., *Tales of the World of Law*, p. 137.
9. Ibid., *Tales of the World of Law*, p. 196.

of administering according to nature." First, he created a dialectic he called "the subtle way of the mutualization of natures," which established his views: "The Spontaneous doing is the special name of the Subtle Way of mutualization of natures. What is the mutualization of natures? It is as follows. Namely, the beginningless and endless Living Truth of earth acts spontaneously, advancing or retreating to greater or lesser degree... untaught and unlearned, neither increasing nor decreasing, it spontaneously does."[10] The mutualization of natures refers to the fact that seemingly opposite things are interdependent, contradictory, and yet unified—and transform into each other through motion. For example, Heaven-and-Earth, the sun and the moon, day and night, light and darkness, man and woman, life and death, old and new, governance and chaos, good and evil, upper and lower, nobility and lowliness, intuition and knowledge, and mentors and disciples. *Symposium* imitates the dialogues in *The Analects* of Confucius (according to his book he was Fujiwara Ryoutyuu, and his disciples called him Master Ryoutyuu), and it records many of Ando's

---

10. Ibid., *The Great Introduction*, pp. 253-254

answers about the mutualization of natures: "The master says: Those who fail to grasp that the Sun and the Moon share mutual natures as one divinity, but instead create their own myths concerning gods born in pairs, male and female, are greatly deluded by a very lopsided intellect. The master says: Those who fail to apprehend that the old and the new share mutual natures and are a single operation of the Living Truth and declare that each day is an utterly new one are deluded by an unbalanced intellect. The master says: Those who do not apprehend that the emotions and the intellect share mutual natures and are the same, single mind, but discuss 'two minds'—a 'mind of the Way' and a 'human mind of desire'—are deluded by an unbalanced intellect. The master says: 'Those who fail to apprehend the Subtle action of the mutual natures of the Way of Energy, and discuss the 'ten stems' and the 'twelve branches' and other calendrical systems, confusing the true seasons of sowing and reaping, are deluded by an unbalanced intellect."[11] Ando used the subtle way of the mutualization of natures to develop an ecological idea of the interdependence of all things, as well as

---

11. Ibid., *Symposium*, pp. 200-202

the concept of equality where "thousands of people are one person" and "man and woman are one person." Based on this, he constructed his utopian World of Self-Acting.

The opposite of the World of Self-Acting is the World of Law, which evolved from the former and will eventually return to it—when "law" will be replaced by "the Way." Ando believed that the World of Self-Acting, prior to the World of Law, was formed through the three "circulations of energy": upward, sideways, and downward. Upward moves downwards, giving birth to humans; sideways is a horizontal movement that forms the ocean, giving birth to birds, beasts, crawling creatures, and fish; downward moves upward, forming land and producing plants and grain. The principles of upward, sideways, and downward also follow the subtle way of the mutualization of natures: Grain (or rice) nourishes people, people grow grain, "people eat grain and produce manure, and grain consumes manure and produces fruits." Grain coexists and co-consumes with people, and both men and women are also "grains." People gather, cultivate, raise animals, and obtain grain, food, and fish. They eat until they are full and are not greedy, and respect the earth and the sea as the parents who feed them. They humbly coexist with all things and have a close connection with nature. In such a World of Self-Acting, everyone shares food and property, helps and supports one other, and there is neither class, competition, nor exploitation. Not only are people equal to each other, but people are equal with plants, animals, the land, the mountains, the rivers and the seas. Before the emergence of humanity, there was only the World of Beasts, as mentioned in *Tales of the World of Law*. After the emergence of humanity, human mutualization of natures transformed the World of Beasts into the World of Self-Acting. But, after the emergence of the "sage," the World of Self-Acting became bestialized and reverted to the World of Beasts again (the World of Law).

In order to return to the World of Self-Acting, Ando called for the emergence of the Right Man, and proposed the idea of Right Cultivation, a term with two distinct meanings. First, it opposes the sage and the privileged class, who "eat greedily without cultivating," and calls on the Right Man to personally engage in labor. Second, it is necessary to carry out correct farming and management in accordance with the mutualization that is inherent in nature. It is necessary to comply with the Five Constants of Nature (birthing, flourishing, harvesting, storing, and transformation) to arrange agricultural work over seasons, while also adhering to the principle of species, land, and climate mutualizing each other—to avoid ecological disasters such as the Wild Boar Famine. If mutualization of natures is the philosophical foundation of *Shizen shin'eido*, then Right Cultivation is its practice, and the Right Man its executor. The ecological thinking reflected in the World of Self-Acting and Right Cultivation are similar to that in permaculture today, which advocates the maintenance of a virtuous cycle ecosystem through the least amount of manpower and the greatest amount of natural forces (sunlight, solar energy, microbial soil, symbiosis, and the mutual nourishing of different species) to achieve agriculturally sustainable development. This principle also applies to the management of human society. The progressiveness of Ando lies in that over 200 years ago he surpassed the concept of ecology first put forward by Ernst Haeckel in 1866, as well as anthropocentric ideas of environmental stewardship—such as protecting the earth for future generations. He directly touched on issues of deep ecology such as animal rights, land justice, and natural rights.

In "A Method for Making the Thieving and Violent World of Law Tally with the World of the Self-acting Living Truth" in *Symposium*, Ando explores the practical path of progressively going from the World of Law to the World of Self-Acting. The editor of Ando's complete works, Terao Goro, refers to this transitional stage of Ando's design as a "World of Compatibility."[12] In a World of Compatibility, Ando holds the supreme position in the World of Law, but only served as "figurehead monarch: ""He must abandon his splendid robes and delicacies of the table, his life lost in luxury, and the pursuit of pleasures and amusements. With no worthless band of followers to support, the amount of land the ruler may claim as his own must be specified and he should then cultivate these lands, feeding

---

[12.] See Terao Goro, "Commentary on the Symposium," in *Complete Works of Ando Shoeki, Vol. 1* (Tokyo: Rural Culture Association Japan, 1984) pp. 171-176.

and clothing his clan with their fruits."[13] Abolish the taxation system and neither reward nor punish, as "If an utterly evil and good-for-nothing person should happen to appear, his family and his clan should put him to death. The ruler should not add any punishment of his own. These affairs are to be matters of the village government, if each clan rights the wrongs of its own members, there will be no evil people."[14] Abolish currency and replace it with barter: "Gold and silver are really nothing more than the fat and gristle of the rocks of the mountains; they are, in other words, nothing but refuse. That is why their use should be abandoned. It will be illegal to sell so much as a single vegetable."[15] Everybody can "cultivate grain and weave cloth throughout their lives. This is the Right Cultivation of the Living Truth among human beings. Heaven-and-Earth are one substance. Neither is ruler or ruled, they have mutual natures and one is not separate from the others. ...In that world there would be no thieving or

---

13. Toshinobu Yasunaga, *Ando Shoeki: Social and Ecological Philosopher in Eighteenth Century Japan* (New York: Weatherhill, 1992), *Symposium*, p. 237.
14. Ibid., p. 245.
15. Ibid., p. 244.

revolt, delusion or strife, for a world where people live in accord with the Way of the Living Truth would be one of peace."[16] According to the idea of "local governance:" "If there were a ruler of human society who was a Right Man, one who understood the Subtle Way of the Living Truth, and he sought to correct human behavior, even this World of Law we live in could become the World of the Living Truth, where all engage in Right Cultivation."[17] This is similar to the statement of Xu Xing, as recorded in the *Mencius* that "the exemplary man works alongside the people and eats what they eat."[18] However, there is no mention of Xu Xing in Ando's works. Yet Xu Xing's School of the Tillers (Nongjia) was regarded by David Graeber as the anarchism of pre-Qin China.[19] His ideas were despised by Confucians

---

16. Ibid., p. 234.
17. Ibid., p. 236.
18. Philip J. Ivanhoe ed., *Mencius*, trans. Irene Bloom (New York: Columbia university Press, 2009), p.54.
19. David Graeber, *Debt: The First 5000 Years* (New York: Melville House, 2012), p. 237.

for attempting to "disrupt the social hierarchy"[20]—but are of the same vein as Ando's criticisms of Confucianism.

Ando's World of Self-Acting was not just utopian primitive communism, nor was it a repetition of Laozi's regression into "a little country without many people."[21] Under the actual conditions of the Edo period, at least a World of Compatibility could be within his grasp. Although the Shogunate's Kanei Isolation Policy lasted from 1633 to 1853, it still allowed for trade with China, Korea, the Ryukyu Kingdom, and the Netherlands. The cultural exchange brought about by international trade also opened Ando's horizons, enabling him to write his seven-volume *The Circulation of Energy in All*

---

20. See Ban Gu, "Treatise on Literature" in the *Book of Han* in Eastern Han Dynasty (25–220 AD): " The first Nongjia may have been agriculture officials who grew different kinds of grain and encouraged people to till land and plant mulberry trees to produce enough food and clothing. Food is so important that it ranks first among the eight major areas of a state's policy, followed by property. The merit of early Nongjia was their emphasis on food production, which Confucius said should be a priority for any ruler. However, their vulgar successors, who believe that a saint-king in the Confucian sense would be useless, attempt to disrupt the social hierarchy by calling on rulers to plough alongside their people."

21. Lao Tzu, *Tao Te Ching: A Book About the Way and the Power of the Way*, trans. Ursula K. Le Guin (Boston: Shambhala Publications,1997), p.111.

Lands, in *Shizen shin'eido*, including his research on Japan, Russia, Korea, China, India, southeast Asian countries, Islamic countries, the Netherlands, and the Ryukyu Kingdom. In his later years, during the height of *Rangaku* (Dutch studies) in Japan (1751-1764), the large number of imported materials deeply interested him in the Netherlands. Through his research, he rated the Netherlands as the "most clean and honest country among all nations." He saw the dawn of the realization of the World of Self-Acting: "From the beginning until now, there has been no war or chaos in the Netherlands, and Right Cultivation has been carried out."[22] His research into other countries also extended his criticism of the World of Law:

"Because of the use of gold and silver as currency, the practice of buying and selling to acquire profit has become widespread. The lust for profit rages throughout the world, and China has, for example, sent expeditions to conquer India, Holland, and Japan; Japan has invaded Korea and conquered the Ryukyu Islands. This has all occurred because

---

[22]. See Jiang Hongsheng, "The Most Clean and Honest Country among All Nations as Heterotopia: Japanese Thinker Ando Shoeki on the Netherlands," *Comparative and World Literature*, Issue 3, 2013.

with the system of commerce based on gold and silver currency, people have been able to acquire whatever they can afford, and are attached to a life of luxury."[23] The idea of free trade as the origin of wars between nations is very close to the pacifist and humanitarian motives of Mushakoji Saneatsu, who devoted himself to the utopia of New Village at the end of World War I.

---

23. Toshinobu Yasunaga, *Ando Shoeki: Social and Ecological Philosopher in Eighteenth Century Japan* (New York: Weatherhill, 1992), *Symposium*, p. 238.

The Tanesashi Coast, Hachinohe.
Photo by Ou Ning, 2019.

THE AGRITOPIAS

Ando, who lived in the 18th century, foreshadowed a large number of ideas that became popular in the 19th and 20th centuries. Right Cultivation can be understood as Tolstoy's pan-laborism, which also bears certain similarities to Mao Zedong's anti-intellectualism during the Cultural Revolution. The *Shizen shin'eido* is a deep well of thought, allowing future generations to take from it what they need. Dialectics, materialism, Marxism, communism, anarchism, utopianism, agriculturalism, deep ecology—and even anti-capitalist and anti-globalization movements can find their own sources in it. More than two hundred years have passed, and the World of Law that Ando opposed seems to have no signs of disappearing or transforming. His ideas were forgotten for over 100 years before being rediscovered at the end of the 19th century. In the 20th century, they were regularly studied and internationally disseminated, but in the 21st century they seem to be in danger of being forgotten again. I have been engaged in the Bishan Project since 2010.[1] Influenced by the Rural Reconstruction Movement in the Republic of China, whose roots I trace back to the New Village Movement led by Mushakoji Saneatsu, I can trace that back to its origin in Japan's agricultural utopianism—all the way from Moroyama to Chofu, Abiko, Hanamaki, and finally to Hachinohe. Unexpectedly, I saw a closure notice at the Ando Shoeki Museum, which I was looking forward to visiting.

The museum is a small and low building, with its own sign hanging on the left side of the entrance and the sign of the local sake brand, Hakkaku, hanging on the right side. It turned out that the museum was also a sake shop. Under the slogan "Hakkaku,

---

[1]. See Ou Ning, *Utopia in Practice: Bishan Project and Rural Reconstruction* (Singapore: Palgrave Macmillan, 2020).

Old Friends," there was a granite sculpture of Ando sitting with a bicycle nearby, adding a more daily feel to the museum. I only arranged my visit according to the usual practice of museums being closed on Mondays, so I didn't expect this museum to be only open for two weeks per month. Looking at their website, the top of the page says "Ando Shoeki: World's First Ecologist." The museum was founded in 2009 and displays mostly replicas. In 2011, it also founded Ando Village in Hachinohe to promote the spirit of Right Cultivation, and provide locals with agricultural experiences. Since the museum wasn't open, I used the map on my mobile phone to search for the remains of Ando's former residence, which showed that it was located nearby. When I finally found the spot, I saw that there were no architectural remains of the Kakuryudo of Ando's medical practice. Instead, scholars had placed a small commemorative pillar there, based on the approximate location of Jusannichi as recorded in historical records. Because there were no more things related to Ando to see, I chose to take a look at the Tanasashi Coast, and like Shiba Ryotaro, I unexpectedly saw the beautiful scenery of

Hachinohe. He wrote about the relationship between Ando's ideas and the cold and harsh climate of the land of Mutsu. For as Ando said, everyone is also "grain," or rice. I call the Japanese utopianists that I was searching for Agritopianists because they all believed in agriculturalism and were all nurtured by East Asian rice culture. Although there are very few traces of Ando left in Hachinohe today, I am still glad to have seen the geographical source of Agritopianists.

From the agricultural utopian philosophy of Ando, to the individual and communal experiments in semi-agricultural life that arose in the late Meiji period, and extending to the Showa period to the Manchukuo migration plan, these all reflect a fervent pursuit of Agritopias in Japan. In addition to the experiments of intellectuals who engaged in half-farming and half-study, some utopian communities of full-time farmers also emerged. During World War II in Kasama Village (in Uda, Nara), Ozaki Masutaro, a member of the new religion, Tenrikyo, was expelled by the religious order due to his suspicions about forced donations. In 1939, he and 18 other companions who had separated from the religious order established the Shinkyo Buraku to independently operate agriculture and practice collective living with shared property. They were investigated by the Japanese authorities due to suspicion of engaging in communist activities. Afterwards, they participated in the agricultural immigration to Manchukuo in 1943. After Japan's defeat in the war in 1945, they returned home and began rebuilding the Shinkyo Buraku the following year. In 1948, they established the Shinkyo Buraku Farm and produced the largest number of tatami mats in Japan at the time. Due to the continued implementation of the collective system and their success in agriculture, they were often referred to as "Japan's Kibbutz."[2] In 1953, Yamagishi Miyozo, who invented a new method of chicken and rice co-cultivation, along with more than 20 followers, started the Yamagishi Association for Happiness. Named after his own surname and located near Kyoto, he interpreted "mountain" (yama) as "ideal" and "shore" (gishi) as "the other shore." They began to promote the "Yamagami doctrine" and

---

[2]. See Nishiyama Taku, "Utopianism in the Thought and Action of Ishikawa Sanshiro."

new agricultural technologies. In 1961, he founded Kasugayama Jikkenchi in Iga, Mie, giving members a place to practice. Afterwards, the Yamagishi Association for Happiness established nearly 40 sites across Japan, and seven more sites in Thailand, South Korea, Australia, Switzerland, the United States, and Brazil. Some sites have over 1000 people living together on them, and their large modern farms have annual sales of five billion yen.[3]

In addition to the overseas expansion of the Yamagishi Association for Happiness due to its successes, Japan's agritopianists also broke through the geographical limitations of being an island country with limited land resources, harsh climate and environmental conditions, and economic crises. They crossed oceans and sought space to live in foreign lands. The colonization of Manchukuo was an aggressive agricultural migration led by the state, but the agritopian movement also erupted in folk society with the immigrants to South America. Japanese immigration to Brazil originated with the

---

[3] See "Over Half a Century of the Yamagishi Association for Happiness," in *Fragrant Soil* magazine, Partnerships for Community Development: https://www.pcd.org.hk/

abolition of the international slave trade at the end of the 19th century. Brazil, which was sparsely populated and needed to replenish labor, issued immigration invitations to both China and Japan. As a result, the Meiji government responded positively and began allowing nationals to immigrate to Brazil in the early 20th century. Initially, the number was not large, but after the Kanto earthquake in 1923, the number surged. In 1926, a 20-year-old Christian baseball player named Yuba Isamu immigrated with his family to the largest Japanese immigrant settlement in Brazil, Fazenda Aliança. In 1935, he proposed the idea of creating a new culture in Brazil's virgin land and, together with seven Japanese immigrant partners, purchased approximately 100 hectares of land in the municipality of Formosa to create Comunidade Yuba. In 1942, Brazil joined the Allied powers in World War II, severed diplomatic relations with Japan, and stopped accepting Japanese immigrants. Despite the absence of new Japanese labor, Comunidade Yuba maintained momentum. It began raising chickens in 1938, and in 1947 became the largest chicken farm in South America, with 220,000 chickens.

Losing contact with their motherland, the Japanese immigrants of Comunidade Yuba had to stick together. They began introducing cultural and artistic activities in 1948 to raise spirits, where people could learn to play the piano, sing, or make instruments by hand. They adhered to the principles of "prayer, cultivation, and art" in their daily lives, and implemented the collective spirit of shared property as well as sharing weal and woe—strengthening the community atmosphere of mutual trust and respect. As a result, it became an isolated overseas Christian socialist agritopia. In 1952, Brazil and Japan resumed diplomatic relations, but with the gradual recovery of the Japanese economy after the war, the number of Japanese immigrants to Brazil would never return to its previous peak. The farm declared bankruptcy in 1956 and was relocated to the village of Aliança in Mirandópolis County, State of São Paulo, for reconstruction. That was approximately 600 kilometers away from the state capital of São Paulo, and half of the original 200 members moved with it. In 1961, sculptor Ohara Hisao and dancer Ohara Akiko joined the farm. Afterwards, the farm built a theater and library, and also established a famous ballet troupe that was invited to tour various parts of Brazil, and later returned to Japan for tours. In 1976, the farm welcomed the visit of Prince Akihito and his wife, making their arduous journey a legend for Japanese cultivation efforts overseas. To today, although Comunidade Yuba has faced difficulties in restructuring the Brazilian-Japanese socio-economic landscape (such as the dissolution of their agricultural association, and the mergers of banks and foreign investment, etc.); their third-generation leaders are still making efforts to maintain their community.[4]

Comunidade Yuba was founded by Yuba Isamu in 1935, New Village was founded by Mushakoji Saneatsu in 1918, and Ittoen was founded by Nishida Tenko in 1904. They are three long-lived agritopias created by the Japanese that still exist today. If both Ittoen and New Village have reached their centennials, Comunidade Yuba is close behind, at almost 90 years old. But compared to the utopia of the *Shizen shin'eido* envisioned by their ancestor

---

[4] The history of Comunidade Yuba can be found on their official website: http://brasil-ya.com/yuba/historia/rekishi_jp.html

Ando Shoeki in 1753, they are relatively young. Agriculture and utopia are two things that attract and sustain each other. A utopia can help agriculture preserve itself from the destruction of nature in the outside world, and resist various emerging enemies that threaten its existence; agriculture can provide material nourishment and economic prosperity to a utopia, as well as an ancient spiritual power and ethical foundation. Haruki Murakami wrote in his novel, *1Q84,* that the success of agriculture gave impetus to the left-wing commune Sakigake deep in the mountains. Historically, many utopian experiments have relied on agriculture for survival, and the combination of the two goes hand in hand. Agritopias exist not only in the dreams of Ando Shoeki but also in the actions of Yuba Isamu. There is a vast Pacific Ocean between the Tanesashi Coast and Formosa, but it has not stopped the resonance of utopian brain waves from traveling across ancient and modern times. As I walked through the pine forests and reefs towards the edge of the ocean, the crashing waves echoed like the thoughts of ghosts, debating loudly.

Translators' Note

It's difficult to remember where we first heard of Ou Ning. Was it from his work as the Chief Editor of the literary magazine *Chutzpah!* (2010-2014), was it his organization of the Bishan Commune (2011-2016), or was it for his early documentary work, *San Yuan Li* (2003)? Or maybe his even earlier book on rock music, *New Sound of Beijing* (1999)? After learning that he had worked for a while at Columbia University (in New York City, where we live), in 2018, Matt sent him an email about two common interests–architecture and poetry. Soon afterwards, we began translating for him—at first, some short essays and talks relating to his Kwan-Yen Project (2015-2018), and then, later on, a large portion of his book *Utopia in Practice: Bishan Project and Rural Reconstruction* (2020). Eventually we translated the present volume, *The Agritopianists: Thinking and Practice in Rural Japan*, which had grown out of his previous studies of intentional communities, combined with recent fieldwork in Japan. This also roughly coincided with Ou Ning's permanent relocation to New York.

Not long after his relocation here, Matt sat on a panel with Ou Ning and a poet that we had translated. There, asked about the difficulty of translating poetry, he said that it really wasn't so hard to do. Turning to his left and looking at Ou Ning, he continued, "translating *this guy* is hard." After which he explained that, unlike much scholarly or nonfiction writing — or poetry — Ou Ning's writing falls between and cuts across many genre conventions, and the particulars of his work pose a number of interesting problems to the translator, including: Who is being spoken to? What register is being used? Where is the line between particularity and abstraction, history and idea? All of these questions become especially pertinent in a book about, ostensibly, idealism. Add to that the fact that Ou Ning's writing is never easy to pin down; it's never an imitation. It is, inimitably, *Ou Ning's language*. So here we are proud to offer another contribution to the growing body of Ou Ning's particular language in English, and to offer additional and important work on the knotty relationship of intentional communities to literary modernism. The labor of translation works outside of monolingual discourse as well as homogeneous societies, and the world of translation is in some ways like an intentional community. Here, its work, once again, asserts itself as a worthwhile endeavor.

Matt Turner and Weng Haiying
02 July, 2024

Glossary

Page numbers in *italics* refer to illustrations.

Abe Yoshishige 安倍能成 , 37
Abiko 我孫子 , *12*, 24-25, *29*, 30-33, 35, 37, 39, 53, 65, *125*, 188, 215
Abuta 虻田 , 150
Aestheticism (Tanbiha) 耽美派 , 21
Agrayana Orbis Mandrus 農乗曼荼羅 , 156
Agricultural Fundamentalism (Nohonshugi) 農本主義 , 136, 138-139, 142, 150, 166-168, 180
Akihito 明仁 , 222
Akita 秋田 , 61, 185-186, 189
Amakasu Incident 甘粕事件 , 28
Amakasu Masahiko 甘粕正彦 , 28
Ando Shoeki 安藤昌益 , *183*, 185-191, *192*, 193-198, 201, 203-212, 214-217, 223
Aomori 青森 , 61, 153, 184
Arahata Kanson 荒畑寒村 , 65
Aranosha 曠野社 , 44, 61, 95, 99
Argument for Leaving Asia (Datsu-A Ron) 脱亜論 , 136
Arima Yoriyasu 有馬頼寧 , 146
Arishima Ikuma 有島生馬 , 16, 32
Arishima Takeo 有島武郎 , 14-16, 20, 26-27, 34, 64, 66-68, 70-71, 74, 177
Arishima Takeshi 有島武 , 67
As Far as Abashiri 『網走まで』, 16
Asahi Shimbun 『朝日新聞』, 2
Asakawa Noritaka 浅川伯教 , 32
Ashigezaki Observatory 葦毛崎展望台 , 185
Ashio Copper Mine 足尾銅山 , 151
Asuka period 飛鳥時代 , 4
Atarashiki-mura 新しき村 , *1*, 3, 4

Baibunsha 売文社 , 154
basic local organizations 基礎的な地方公共団体 , 5
Boatmen's Forest (Funato no Mori) 船戸の森 , 36
Buji 『不二』, 28
Buraku Liberation League 部落解放同盟 , 67-68

Campaign for Imperial Rural Establishment 皇国農村確立運動 , 146, 165
Chiba 千葉 , 27, 119
Chichibu 秩父 , 10
Chikuma Shobo 筑摩書房 , 19, 178
Chitose 千歳 , 152-153, 162
cho/machi 町 , 5
chonin 町人 , 194
Civic News (*Heimin Shinbun*) 『平民新聞』, 166, 186
Comunidade Yuba 弓場農場 , 220-222

dan 石 , 195
Dewa Province 出羽國 , 189
do 道 , 5

Ebara 荏原, 160
Edo period 江戸時代, 14, 185-186, 193, 195, 210
Eguchi Kiyoshi 江口渙, 64
Emperor Ninko 仁孝天皇, 14
Emperor Saga 嵯峨天皇, 14
Empress Danrin 檀林皇后, 14
Eto Tekirei 江渡狄嶺, 153-157, 162, 187

Farmers' Training Ground of Love (Hyakusho Aidojo) 百姓愛道場, 154
Fazenda Aliança 農場連盟, 220
Feldologie 田野学, 155
figurehead monarch 虚君, 207
Fujisawa 藤沢, 15
Fujiwara Ryoutyuu 藤原良中, 186, 202
Fukao Sho 深尾韶, 150
Fukuoka 福岡, 25, 61
Fukushima 福島, 43
Fukuzawa Yukichi 福沢諭吉, 136
Funabashi 船橋, 153, 162
fu 府, 5

gabled roof construction (kirizuma-zukuri) 切妻造, 109
Gakushuin 学習院, 14
Gakushujo 学習所, 14
Ganei Temple 願栄寺, 189
Gassho『合掌』, 74
Gassho-style houses (Gassho-zukuri) 合掌造, 33
Genroku 元禄, 191, 193
Gifu 岐阜, 61
Ginza 銀座, 38
Gondo Seikyo 権藤成卿, 139, 143-145, 155, 164
go 合, 44
Greater East Asia Co-Prosperity Sphere (Daitoa kyoeiken) 大東亜共栄圏, 137-138, 141-142, 145, 153
Gunma 群馬, 14, *124*

Hachiko 八高線, *1*, 3
Hachinohe 八戸, *183*, 185-186, 189-190, *192*, 194-195, *213*, 215-217
Hachioji 八王子, 10
haiku poet 俳人, 152
Hakkaku 八鶴, 215
hakko ichiu 八紘一宇, 142
Hakodate 函館, 61
Hamada Shoji 濱田庄司, 32
Hamamatsu 浜松, 25, 61
Hanamaki Agricultural High School 花巻農学校, *149*, 161, *169*, 171-172, 176, 179
Hanamaki 花巻, *149*, 161, *169*, 170-173, 176, 179, 181, 215
Hara Neki 原子基, 150
Hasegawa Nyozekan 長谷川如是閑, 157
Hashimoto Denzaemon 橋本伝左衛門, 157
Hasimoto Rituzou 橋本律蔵, 186
Hata Nobuko 羽太信子, 106
Hatano Akiko 波多野秋子, 27

Heian Period 平安時代, 14
Hidaka 日高, 122
Higashi-Moro 東毛呂, 2
High Treason Incident (Taigyaku Jiken) 大逆事件, 17, 19, 64, 153, 166
Hirabayashi Hatsunosuke 平林初之輔, 64
Hirata Tosuke 平田東助, 139
Hiroshige Utagawa 歌川廣重, 185
Hiroshima 広島, 61
Hirotsu Kazuo 広津和郎, 73
Historia Regionalis 地方学, 155
Hokkaido 北海道, 67, 69, 75, 142, 150
Hokkeshu 法華宗, 181-182
Hokuto 北杜, 38
home schooling 自宅教育, 157
Honma Hisao 本間久雄, 64
House of Peers (Kizoku In) 貴族院, 106
Hyuga 日向, 4, 25, 55

Ibaraki 茨城, 163
Iburinokuni 膽振國, 67
Iga 伊賀, 219
Iida Momo 飯田桃, 191, 195
Ikebukuro 池袋, 2
Imperial Way Faction (Kodoha) 皇道派, 104
Inamura Ryuichi 稲村隆一, 143
Inatori 稲取, 165
Inoue Junnosuke 井上準之助, 164
Inoue Nissho 井上日召, 164, 181
Inukai Ken 犬養健, 37
Inukai Tsuyoshi 犬養毅, 66, 103, 164
Inuta Shigeru 犬田卯, 143
Iruma 入間, 2, 109
Ishiguro Tadaatsu 石黒忠篤, 139
Ishikawa Sanshiro 石川三四郎, 74, 162, 164-167, 172, 218
Ishikawa Takuboku 石川啄木, 20-21
Ishikawauchi 石河内, 41-42, 57
Ishiwara Kanji 石原莞爾, 103, 181
Isimura Seimei 石村清明, 118
Ito Isao 伊藤勇雄, 120
Ito Noe 伊藤野枝, 27
Ittoen 一燈園, 75-76, 222
Iwanami Shoten 岩波書店, 15, 136, 187
Iwate 岩手, 120, 161, 170, 176-179, 184
Iwato Boom 岩戸景気, 114-115
Izanagi Boom いざなぎ景気, 115

Japan Folk Crafts Museum 日本民藝館, 2, 32
Japan-Korea Annexation Treaty 韓国併合ニ関スル條約, 17
Jikkenchi 実顕地, 219
Jimbo Village 神保町, 118
Joban 常磐, 163
Jogetsuan 浄月庵, 27
jo 畳, 44

Judo 柔道, 31
Jusannichi 十三日町, 189, *192*, 216

Kadenokoji Sukekoto 勘解由小路資承, 13
Kadenokoji Yasuko 勘解由小路康子, 35, 52
Kadokawa 角川, 113
Kagoshima 鹿児島, 43
Kakuryudo 鎌竜堂, 186, 216
Kamakura 鎌倉, 30-31
Kamata 蒲田, 160
Kameido 亀戸, 163
Kami-Takaido 上高井戸, 154
Kamiyama Senakira 神山仙確, 190
Kanagawa 神奈川, 15, 27, 102
Kanei Isolation Policy (Kanei Sakoku) 寛永鎖國令, 210
Kaneko Yobun 金子洋文, 64-65
Kano Jigoro 嘉納治五郎, 31, 33
Kano Kokichi 狩野亨吉, 185-187
Kanto Great Earthquake 関東大地震, 61, 137
Kanto Region 関東地方, 5, 163
Kaributo 狩太, 67-68, 70-71, 158
Karuizawa 軽井沢町, 27
Kasama 笠間, 217
Kasugayama 春日山, 219
Kasuya 粕谷, 152
Katayama Sen 片山潜, 165
Kato Kanji 加藤完治, 140, 147
Kato Kazuo 加藤一夫, 64, 140, 143, 165
Kawai Kanjiro 河井寛次郎, 32
Kawakami Hajime 河上肇, 64, 139
Kawaminami 川南, 61
Kazoku Gakko (Peers School) 華族学校, 14-15, 18-19, 54, 67
Kazoku 華族, 13-14
ken 県, 5
Ketsumeidan 血盟団, 164
Kijo 木城, 4, 6, 25, 36, 41-44, 54-55, 58-61, 104, 112, 114, 119, *126*, *129-131*, 160
Kikuchi Hiroshi 菊池寛, 73
Kimura Hiroshi 木村博, 156
Kimura Syouta 木村庄太, 55-57, 94, 119
Kinoshita Rigen 木下利玄, 15-16
Kishida Ryusei 岸田劉生, 26, 37, 60
Kita Ikki 北一輝, 181
Kitakami River 北上川, 179
Kitakami Valley 北上盆地, 170
Kitano Tenmangu Shrine 北野天満宮, 189
Kitatama 北多摩, 112, 152
Kitatoshima 北豊島, 44
Kiyama Kumazi 木山熊次, 186
Kiyoharu Art Colony 清春芸術村, 38
Kiyoharu Shirakaba Museum 清春白樺美術館, 38
Kobayashi Takiji 小林多喜二, 31, 102-103
Kobayashi Tatsue 小林多津衛, 119
Kobe 神戸, 25, 61

Kobun Institute 弘文學院 , 31
Kodaira Hideo 小平英男 , 154
Kodansha 讲谈社 , 51, 102-103
Kodera Kenkichi 小寺謙吉 , 138
Koga Kiyoshi 古賀清志 , 164
Kohno Michisei 河野通勢 , 8
Koide Manji 小出満二 , 157
Kojima Kikuo 児島喜久雄 , 16
Kokuchukai 國柱會 , 181-182
Komaba 駒場 , 2, 32
Kon Toko 今東光 , 143
Konoe Fumimaro 近衞文麿 , 137
Kori Torahiko 郡虎彦 , 15-16
Koromo 挙母 , 61
Kotoku Shusui 幸徳秋水 , 17-20, 63, 153, 166, 186
Koyu 児湯 , 4, 25
Kurata Hyakuzo 倉田百三 , 8, 74-75
Kura 十藏 , 154
Kure 呉市 , 61
Kurosawa Teijiro 黒沢貞次郎 , 160
Kyushu 九州 , 4, 157

Lake Teganuma 手賀沼 , 33, 36
land tax reform (*chisokaisei*) 地租改正 , 140
Levelers Association (Suiheisha) 水平社 , 67
Lotus Sutra (*Saddharma Pundarika Sutra*)『妙法蓮華経』, 181

Maeda Masana 前田正名 , 139
Makkari Village 真狩村 , 150
Matsumae 松前 , 190
Matsumoto 松本 , 25
Meguro 目黒 , 2, 32
Meiji Emperor 明治天皇 , 17, 19, 21
Meiji Restoration 明治維新 , 23, 137, 139, 140-141
Meiji 明治 , 4, 13-17, 19, 21, 23, 49, 135, 137, 139-141, 172, 185-186, 217, 220
Meshigawa Yasuko 飯河安子 , 58, 109
Mie 三重 , 219
Mikasa 三笠 , 27
Mingei 民藝 , 32
Minka 民家 , 110, 172
miso 味噌 , 179
Mitaka 三鷹 , 112
Mito 水戸 , 163
Miyagi 宮城県 , 184
Miyawaki Junko 宮脇淳子 , 23
Miyazaki 宮崎 , 4, 25, 43, 57-59, 61
Miyazawa Kenji Dowa Mura 宮沢賢治童話村 , 170-171
Miyazawa Kenji Ihatov Center 宮沢賢治イーハトーブ館 , 171
Miyazawa Kenji Museum 宮沢賢治記念館 , 170, 173
Miyazawa Kenji 宮沢賢治 , *149*, 161, 164, 166, *169*, 170-171, 173, 176-178, 180, 182
Miyazawa Kisuke 宮沢喜助 , 161
Miyazawa Masajiro 宮沢政次郎 , 180

Mizuno Yoshu 水野葉舟, 154
Mojiko Station 門司港, 43
Morioka 盛岡, 179
Moroyama 毛呂山, 2, 4-5, 7, 10-11, *40*, 42, 59, *62*, 104, *111*, 112-115, 117-118, 120-122, *123*, *131-134*, 215
Mount Akagi 赤城山, 14, *124*
Mount Ashitaka 愛鷹山, 163
Mount Fuji 富士山, 14, *124*, 163
Mount Osuzu 尾鈴山, 41
Municipalities of Japan (Shichoson) 市町村, 4
Murakami Haruki 村上春樹, 223
Murayama Shoho 村山祥峰, 33
Murobuse Takanobu 室伏高信, 157
Musashino 武蔵野, 152
Mushakoji Kintomo 武者小路公共, 104
Mushakoji Saneatsu and Atarashiki-mura Memorial Museum 武者小路実篤記念新しき村美術館, *1*, 3
Mushakoji Saneatsu Memorial Museum in Chofu 調布市武者小路実篤記念館, 8, 54-55, *98*, 109, *124-133*
Mushakoji Saneatsu 武者小路実篤, *1*, 3-10, 13-16, 18-19, 24-28, *29*, 30-31, 35-39, 42-45, 49-56, 58-61, *62*, 63-66, 71-74, 76, *77*, 81-82, 85-87, 91, 93-96, *98*, 99-110, *111*, 112-115, 117-119, *124-133*, 138, 143, 152-153, 158-159, 171, 177, 179, 188, 212, 215, 222
Mushakoji Saneyo 武者小路実世, 13
Mutsu Province 陸奥國, 189
Mutual Learning Association (Kyougakusha) 共学社, 162, 165
Myoshinji Temple 妙心寺, 189

Nagano Akira 長野朗, 139, 143
Nagano 長野, 26-27, 61, 143
Nagasaka 長坂, 38
Nagasaki 長崎, 194
Nagayo Yoshiro 長與善郎, 8, 19, 27, 37, 60, 73, 109
Nakagawa Kazumasa 中川一政, 8
Nakajima Kaneko 中島兼子, 31, 34
Nakazato Kaizan 中里介山, 154
Nakazawa Benjiro 中沢弁次郎, 143
Nara 奈良, 60, 217
Nasu Shiroshi 那須皓, 140
National Spiritual Mobilization Movement 國民精神總動員, 146
Natsume Soseki 夏目漱石, 16
Naturalism (Shizenshugi) 自然主義, 21
New Idealism (Shinrisoshugi) 新理想主義, 16, 21
New Realism (Shingenjitsushugi) 新現実主義, 28
Nichi Nichi Shimbun 日日新聞社, 58
Nichiren Buddhism 日蓮宗, 181
Niida 二井田, 189-190
Niigata 新潟, 61
Ninomiya Sontoku 二宮尊徳, 140
Nirayama Keisuke 韮山圭介, 119
Niseko 新雪谷, 67
Nishida Tenko 西田天香, 76, 222
Nishimura Shunichi 西村俊一, 157

Nishiyama Taku 西山拓 , 74, 165, 218
Nogi Maresuke 乃木希典 , 19
Nozono『望野』, 15

Oda Makoto 小田実 , 122
Odate 大館 , 185-186, 189
Ogimachi Kinkazu 正親町公和 , 15-16
Ogyu Sorai 荻生徂徠 , 140
Ohara Akiko 小原明子 , 221
Ohara Hisao 小原久雄 , 221
Ohara Magosaburo 大原孫三郎 , 160
Ohara Yugaku 大原幽学 , 140
Okada Narau 岡田温 , 139
Okamoto Rikichi 岡本利吉 , 143, 162, 164
Okawa Shumei 大川周明 , 138
Okayama 岡山 , 61
Olympic Boom オリンピック景気 , 115
Omaru River 小丸川 , 41-42, 54, 58
Omi Komaki 小牧近江 , 64
Ono Takeo 小野武夫 , 143
Osaka Daily News (Osaka Mainichi Shimbun)『大阪毎日新聞』, 25, 57
Oshika hanto 牡鹿半島 , 184
Osugi Sakae 大杉栄 , 27, 64, 81, 164, 166
Otaru University of Commerce 小樽商科大学 , 31
Otaru 小樽 , 31, 61, 70
Oyama Hachisaburo 大山八三郎 , 122
Ozaki Kihachi 尾崎喜八 , 154
Ozaki Masutaro 尾崎増太郎 , 217

Personal Thoughts on the Great East Asia War『大東亜戦争私感』, 105
Prefectures of Japan (Todofuken) 都道府県 , 4
promotion of industry (*shokusan-kogyo*) 殖産興業 , 140
Provinces of Japan (Ryoseikoku) 令制国 , 4
Pure Land Buddhism (Jodo Shinshu) 浄土真宗 , 180

Rakuyodo 洛陽堂 , 15
Rangaku 蘭学 , 211
Rasuchijin Association (Rasu chijin kyokai) 羅須地人協会 , *149*, 161, *169*, 170-172, 177, 179
Revive Asia Society (Koa kai) 興亜会 , 138
Rice Riots (Kome Sodo) 米騒動 , 23, 24, 65
Right Cultivation 直耕 , 190, 198, 205-206, 208-209, 211, 214, 216
Right Man 正人 , 205-206, 209
Rikuchu Kaigan 陸中海岸 , 179
Rural Culture Association Japan 農山漁村文化協会 , 146, 187, 189, 207
Rural Economic Revitalization Campaign 農山漁村経済更生運動 , 145-146, 157, 165
Ryoma Sakamoto 坂本龍馬 , 122
Ryukyu Kingdom 琉球国 . 210

Saikensha 再建社 , 51
Saiki 佐伯 , 61
Saitama 埼玉 , 2-3

Sakado 坂戸, 2
Sakai Toshihiko 堺利彦, 63, 65, 154, 166
Sakakura Junzo 坂倉準三, 109
Sakamoto Syou 坂本尚, 195
Sakigake 先駆, 223
Sanjuso 三樹荘, 33
Sankyo Frontier 三協前線集團, 37
Sano Kei 佐野契, 34
Sano Riki 佐野力, 31
Sanriku Coast 三陸海岸, 184, 194
Sapporo Agricultural College (Sapporo no Gakko) 札幌農学校, 67
Sato Haruo 佐藤春夫, 74
Satomi Ton 里見弴, 15-16, 19
Sazi Masahiro 佐治正大, 34
Sekimura Miki 関村ミキと, 154
Sengawa 仙川, 109
Senge Motomaro 千家元麿, 8, 27
se 畝, 44
shaku 勺, 44
Shiba Ryotaro 司馬遼太郎, 185, 216
Shiga Naoya 志賀直哉, 14-16, 18-19, 27-28, 30-33, 33-37, 52, 60, 73, 109, *124*, *128*
Shigeho Mera 米良重穂, 119, *126*
Shimonaka Yasaburo 下中彌三郎, 143
Shimo-Takaido 下高井戸, 8, 154
Shinagawa Yajiro 品川弥二郎, 139
Shinjuku 新宿, 2
Shinkyo Buraku 心境部落, 218
Shinomiyayanagiyama 四ノ宮柳山, 75
Shinshu 信州, 26
Shinto 神道, 19, 138, 147, 189, 196, 200
Shiomi Naoki 塩見直紀, 121
Shirakaba Literary Museum 白樺文学館, 12, 30, 33
Shirakaba『白樺』, 8, 15-16, 18, 25-28, 32, 43, 52-53, *128*
Shizen shin'eido『自然眞營道』, 186-190, 196, 202, 206, 211, 214, 222
Shizuoka 静岡, 27, 163, 165
shi 市, 5
Shogakukan 小学館, 44, 61
Showa 昭和, 4, 13, 101, 135-137, 139, 142-143, 162, 164, 168, 170, 184, 217
shrine (*shinsha*) 神社, 138
Shunga 春画, 188
Society of Commoners (Heiminsha) 平民社, 63, 143, 150-151, 158, 166
son/mura 大字, 5
Soto Zen 曹洞宗, 154
Subtle Way of Mutualization of Natures 互性妙道, 202-204
Sugawara no Michizane 菅原道眞, 189
Sugiyama Masao 杉山正雄, 58
Sukiya style (Sukiya-zukuri) 数寄屋造り, 109
Susono 裾野, 163
Syndikatologie 総体論, 155

Tachibana Kozaburo 橘孝三郎, 139, 143, 163-164, 166
Tachibana no Kachiko 橘嘉智子, 14
Tachibana Soichi 橘宗一, 27-28

Taisei Yokusankai Movement 大政翼賛会運動, 146-147
Taisho 大正, 4, 8, 21, 26, 30, 49, 65, 101, 135-136, 139, 165, 170
Taizan kiln (Taizangama) 泰山窯, 116
Takachio Chiyo 高知尾智燿, 181
Takajo 高城, 43
Takamura Kotaro 高村光太郎, 154
Takanabe 高鍋, 43
Takata Hiroatsu 高田博厚, 8, 154
Takata Yasuma 高田保馬, 64
Takeo Fusako 竹尾房子, 24, 52, 56, 58-59
Tanabe Kiyoshi 田辺潔, 102
Tanaka Chigaku 田中智學, 181
Tanesashi Coast 種差海岸, 184-185, *213*, 223
Tani Tateki 谷干城, 139
tan 反, 44
Tarui Tokichi 樽井藤吉, 138
Tatologie 互変論, 155
Tawaramono (dried marine products) 俵物, 194
Teiichi Sakuma 佐久間貞一, 160
Tenchi Zendo 天地禅堂, 154
Tenjinyama Ryokuchi Park 天神山緑地, 33
Tenjinzaka 天神坂, 33
Tenshoji Temple 天聖寺, 190
Tensyoudou 天正堂, 186
Terao Goro 寺尾五郎, 207
The Sower (*Tane maku Hito*) 『種蒔く人』, 64
Theory of Asian Federation (Tongyang yondaeron) 東洋連帯論, 136
Theory of Great Eastern Federation 大東合邦論, 138
Three Convolvuluses Farm (Santsuta) 三蔦苑, 154, 156-158
Tobukimachi 戸吹町, 10
Toden 都電, 10
Todo shinden『統道真伝』, 189
Tohoku Region 東北地方, 142-143
Tokko police (Tokubetsu Koto Keisatsu) 特殊高等警察, 102
Tokugawa shogunate 徳川幕府, 189
Tokutomi Kenjiro 徳冨健次郎, 151-152, 162
Tokutomi Roka 徳冨蘆花, 151
Tokutomi Soho 徳冨蘇峰, 138, 153
Tokyo Kogensha 東京光原社, 177
Tomioka 富岡, 163
Toryo Shuppanbu 杜陵出版部, 177
Toseiha (Control Faction) 統制派, 104
Toyama 遠山, 119
to 都, 5
Tsubaki Sadao 椿貞雄, 8
tsubo 坪, 44
Tsuzuranuki 葛貫, 5

Ubukata Naokichi 幼方直吉, 20
Uchida Yoshikazu 内田祥三, 147
Uchimura Kanzo 内村鑑三, 166
Uda 宇陀, 217
Ueda Shin 上田信, 195

Ukiyo-e 浮世絵, 32, 185, 188
Umehara Ryuzaburo 梅原龍三郎, 37
Utida 内田, 186

Wago Tsuneo 和合恒男, 143
Wakaba 若葉, 109
Wakayama 和歌山, 32
Watanabe Kanezirou 渡邊兼次郎, 116
Watanabe Kanji 渡辺貫二, 60
Watanabe Kanzi 渡邊貫二, *111*, 118
Watanabe Osamu 渡邊修, 116
Watanabe Shotaro 渡邊正太郎, 150
Wheel of Home Farming 家稼農乗学, 155-156
White Birch Society (Shirakaba-ha) 白樺派, 15, 17-21, 24-28, 30-34, 36-38, 53, 56, 60, 64, 67, 73-74, 102, *125*, 164
wide-area regional organizations 広域の地方公共団体, 5
Wild Boar Famine 猪饑饉, 195, 201, 206
Women's Review (Fujin Koron)『婦人公論』, 27
World of Law 法世, 196, 200-201, 204-205, 207, 209, 211, 215
World of Self-Acting 自然世, 204-207, 210-211

Yamada Hukuo 山田福男, 187
Yamagata Aritomo 山縣有朋, 19, 65
Yamagishi Association for Happiness 山岸会, 218-219
Yamagishi Miyozo 山岸巳代蔵, 218
Yamaguchi 山口, 61
Yamaguti Hosyun 山口芳春, 109
Yamakawa Hitoshi 山川均, 63, 65-66
Yamamoto Koyata 山本顧彌太, 60
Yamanashi 山梨, 14, 38, *124*
Yamanouchi Hideo 山内英夫, 15
Yamazaki Nobuyoshi 山崎延吉, 139
Yanagi Kaneko 柳兼子, 31, 34
Yanagi Soetsu 柳宗悦, 15-16, 19-20, 26, 30-32, 35-37, 60, 73, 109, *128*
Yanagita Kunio 柳田國男, 139
Yanaka 谷中, 151
Yasukawa Sadao 安川定男, 20
Yasunaga Toshinobu 安永寿延, 187, 191, 198, 208, 212
Yokohama 横浜, 61
Yokoi Kunisaburou 横井国三郎, 57
Yokoi Tokiyoshi 横井時敬, 139
Yomiuri Shimbun『読売新聞』, 5, 42, 167
Yonechi Fumio 米地文夫, 176-177
Yoruzuchoho『萬朝報』, 19
Yoshii Chozo 吉井長三, 38
Yoshii Gallery 吉井画廊, 38
Yoshimatsu 吉松, 43
Yuba Isamu 弓場勇, 220, 222
Yukio Akimiti 三島章道, 54-55

References

Amazawa, Taijiro. *Photo Collection: The World of Miyazawa Kenji*. Tokyo: Chikuma Shobo, 1996.

Baruma, Ian. *Inventing Japan: 1853-1964*. New York: The Modern Library, 2004.

Chen, Zishan and Zhang, Tierong (eds.). *Zhou Zuoren Uncollected Works*. Haikou: Hainan International Press and Publication Center, 1995.

China Li Dazhao Research Association (ed.). *The Complete Works of Li Dazhao*. Beijing: People's Publishing House, 2006.

Chinese Academy of Culture (ed.). *Complete Works of Liang Shuming*, vol. 5. Jinan: Shandong People's Publishing House, 1992.

Saneatsu Mushanokōji Memorial Museum (ed.). *Chofu Saneatsu Mushanokōji Memorial Museum Catalog*. Chofu: Saneatsu Mushanokōji Memorial Museum, 1994.

Curley, Melissa Anne-Marie. "Fruit, Fossils, Footprints: Cathecting Utopia in the Work of Miyazawa Kenji", in Daniel Boscaljon (ed.), *Hope and the Longing for Utopia: Futures and Illusions in Theology and Narrative*. Eugene: Pickwick Publications, 2014, pp. 96-118.

Dong, Bingyue. "The Last Oasis: Japan's New Village Today." *21st Century* 88 (April 2005).

E. H. Norman. *Ando Shoeki and the Anatomy of Japanese Feudalism*. Tokyo: The Asiatic Society of Japan, 1949.

Freire, Paulo. *Pedagogy in Process: The Letters to Guinea-Bissau*. New York: Seabury Press, 1977.

Gao, Hua. *How the Red Sun Rose*. Hong Kong: Chinese University Press, 2000.

Graeber, David. *Debt: The First 5000 Years*. New York: Melville House, 2012.

Hu, Shih. *Collected Essays of Hu Shih*. Beijing: Capital Economic and Trade University Press, 2013.

Jiang, Hongsheng. "The Most Clean and Honest Country among All Nations as Heterotopia: Japanese Thinker Ando Shoeki on the Netherlands." *Comparative and World Literature* 3 (2013).

Johnson, Paul. *Intellectuals: From Marx and Tolstoy to Sartre and Chomsky*. New York: Harper Collins, 2007.

Kimura, Hiroshi. "The Wheel of Home Farming and Theory of Rural Reconstruction: Eto Tekirei and Liang Shuming," *Comparative Thought* 26 (March 2000).

Kropotkin, Peter. *The Conquest of Bread and Other Writings*. Cambridge: Cambridge University Press, 1995.

Liu, Feng. "The Relevance of Modern Japanese Agricultural Fundamentalism and Asianism," *World History* 231(2015).

Liu, Lishan. *Japanese Writers of the White Birch Society and Chinese Writers*. Shenyang: Liaoning University Press, 1995.

Meng, Qingyan. "Diggers and Agitators: On the Peasant Movement in the Early Rural Revolution of the Communist Party," *Society* 37 (2017).

Miyazawa, Kenji. *Outline of the Theory of the Farmers' Art*. Hanamaki: Hanamaki Cultural Group Council, 2018.

Morris-Suzuki, Tessa. "Beyond Utopia: New Villages and Living Politics in Modern Japan and across Frontiers," in *History Workshop Journal* 85 (2018).

Mushakoji Saneatsu Memorial Museum (ed.). *100 Years of New Village: 1918-2018*. Chofu: Saneatsu Mushanokōji Memorial Museum, 2018.

Mushakoji, Saneatsu. *Biography of Buddha*. Kodansha, 1934.

Mushakoji, Saneatsu. *Biography of Jesus*. New Village Publishing, 1920.

Mushakoji, Saneatsu. *Biography of Tolstoy*. Saikensha, 1959.

Mushakoji, Saneatsu. *Selected Works of Mushakoji Saneatsu*. Tokyo: Sedousha, 1964.

Mushakoji, Saneatsu. *The Complete Works of Mushakoji Saneatsu*. Tokyo: Shogakukan, 1988.

Mushakoji, Saneatsu. *The Land*. Tokyo: Aranosha, 1921.

Mushakoji, Saneatsu. *The Life of New Village*. Tokyo: Shinchosha, 1918.

Mushakoji, Saneatsu. Sun Baigang (tr.). *New Village*. Shanghai: Guanghua Book Company, 1933.

Nishimura, Shunichi. "Liang Shuming's Theory of Comparative Thought, and Educational Practice: A Comparative Study with Japanese Rural Educator Eto Tekirei," *International Education* 21 (March 2001).

Nishiyama, Taku. "Utopianism in the Thought and Action of Ishikawa Sanshiro: The Theory of the Ideal Society and Social Reform by the Intellectual in Modern Japan," Waseda University dissertation, Graduate School of Social Sciences, 2009. Waseda University Repository: https://waseda.repo.nii.ac.jp

Schram, Stuart (ed.). John King Fairbank Center (tr.). *Mao's Road to Power: Revolutionary Writings, 1912-49*. New York: M.E. Sharpe, 1992.

Shiomi, Naoki. Su Fengya (tr.). *The Life of Half-Agriculture and Half-X: Follow Nature and Practice Talent*. Taipei: Commonwealth Publishing, 2006.

Shirakaba (reproductions). Kyoto: Rinsen Shoten, 1965.

Terao, Goro (ed.). *Complete Works of Ando Shoeki, Vol. 1*. Tokyo: Rural Culture Association Japan, 1984.

Tokutomi, Kenjiro. *The Babble of Earthworms*. Tokyo: Shinbashido Shoten, 1913.

Ueda, Shin. Gao Yingying (tr.). *The Sea and Empire: Ming and Qing Dynasties*. Guilin: Guangxi Normal University Press, 2014.

Wang, Shouhua and Li, Caihua (eds.). *Ando Shoeki · Modern · China: Collection of the Sino-Japanese Ando Shoeki Academic Symposium*. Jinan: Shandong People's Publishing House, 1993.

Wang, Shouhua (ed.). *Ando Shoeki Research Material Index*. Jinan: Department of Philosophy, Shandong University, 1985.

Yasunaga, Toshinobu (ed.). Yamada Hukuo (photographer). *Photobook: Ando Shoeki*. Tokyo: Rural Culture Association Japan, 1987.

Yasunaga, Toshinobu. *Ando Shoeki: Social and Ecological Philosopher in Eighteenth Century Japan*. New York: Weatherhill, 1992.

Yonechi, Fumio. "A Geographical Study of the Origin and Changes in the Toponym 'Ihatov' Created by Miyazawa Kenji," *Annual Journal of the Iwate University Faculty of Education* 55 (1996).

Zhao, Hong. *The Chinese Dream of a New Village*. Guiyang: Guizhou People's Publishing House, 2014.

Zhou, Zuoren. *Art and Life*. Beijing: October Literature and Art Press, 2011.

Copyright @ Ou Ning
English translation copyright @ Center for Arts,
Design, and Social Research, Inc.

All rights reserved

ISBN 978-1-7356981-1-3

Production: Isogloss, Inc.
Printed in JKL United Printing, Shenzhen, China

www.centerartsdesign.org

A publication of the Center for Arts, Design, and Social Research, 2024
Editors: Dalida María Benfield and Christopher Bratton